A Practical Guide to Teaching Modern Foreign Languages in the Secondary School

A Practical Guide to Teaching Modern Foreign Languages in the Secondary School offers valuable support for student teachers and teachers in their early professional development. It complements and extends the successful companion to school experience, *Learning to Teach MFL in the Secondary School*, and covers a wide range of topics of direct relevance to foreign language education including:

- dominant methodological approaches to foreign language teaching;
- how best to use the target language as a medium for instruction and interaction;
- planning and assessment;
- teaching the four language skills - listening, speaking, reading and writing;
- practical approaches to the teaching of grammar, and the role of cultural awareness;
- building on the foundations laid in primary schools;
- working with other adults in the classroom;
- your own professional development through teacher research.

The chapters illustrate good practice and provide detailed guidance on everyday pedagogical challenges; importantly, they are also grounded in the latest professional writing in the field.

Working through the material presented here will enable you to reach specific objectives in relation to teaching modern foreign languages in the secondary school, by engaging with specific aspects of subject knowledge and pedagogical practice at a conceptual level, as well as with tasks designed to support your learning. In this way the book introduces a range of tried and tested approaches, designed to support your development in MFL teaching.

Norbert Pachler is Associate Dean: Initial and Continuing Professional Development and Co-Director of the Centre for Excellence in Work-based Learning for Education Professionals at the Institute of Education, University of London. He was previously Subject Leader for the Secondary PGCE in Modern Foreign Languages and Course Leader for the MA in Modern Languages in Education.

Ana Redondo is Lecturer in Education in the School of Culture, Language and Communication at the Institute of Education, University of London. She is currently a part-time tutor on the Secondary PGCE in Modern Foreign Languages, and is also a part-time Head of Modern Languages and Senior Teacher at a London secondary school.

Routledge Teaching Guides
Series Editors: Susan Capel and Marilyn Leask

These Practical Guides have been designed as companions to **Learning to Teach (subject) in the Secondary School**. For information on the Routledge Teaching Guides series please visit our website at www.routledge.com/education.

Other titles in the series:

A Practical Guide to Teaching Physical Education in the Secondary School
Edited by *Susan Capel, Peter Breckon and Jean O'Neill*

A Practical Guide to Teaching History in the Secondary School
Edited by *Martin Hunt*

A Practical Guide to Teaching Citizenship in the Secondary School
Edited by *Liam Gearon*

A Practical Guide to Teaching ICT in the Secondary School
Steve Kennewell

A Practical Guide to Teaching Modern Foreign Languages in the Secondary School

Edited by
Norbert Pachler and Ana Redondo

Routledge
Taylor & Francis Group

LONDON AND NEW YORK

First published 2007 by Routledge
2 Park Square, Milton Park, Abingdon, Oxon OX14 4RN

Simultaneously published in the USA and Canada
by Routledge
711 Third Ave, New York, NY 10017

Routledge is an imprint of the Taylor & Francis Group, an informa business

© 2007 Norbert Pachler and Ana Redondo for editorial matter and selection.
Individual chapters, the contributors.

Typeset in Palatino and Frutiger by
Keystroke, 28 High Street, Tettenhall, Wolverhampton

British Library Cataloguing in Publication Data
A catalogue record for this book is available from the British Library

Library of Congress Cataloging in Publication Data
A catalog record for this book has been requested

ISBN10: 0-415-39328-0 (pbk)
ISBN10: 0-203-96801-8 (ebk)

ISBN13: 978-0-415-39328-7 (pbk)
ISBN13: 978-0-203-96801-7 (ebk)

372.65
PR

Contents

Contributors

Ann Barnes leads the Secondary PGCE programme at the University of Warwick and coordinates the MFL strand. Her research interests focus on the development of student teachers in modern languages, assessment in MFL and primary languages. She has published numerous articles, chapters and books in theses areas. Ann taught in 11–18 and post-16 institutions before moving in to teacher education and supervises a number of research students.

Verna Brandford is a Lecturer in Education at the Institute of Education, University of London where she works as a tutor on the Secondary PGCE in Modern Foreign Languages. She is also an Institute Partnership Manager and she oversees the Secondary Part time Professional Studies Course. She has taught in and trained language teachers for primary and secondary schools as well as adult education. As a consultant MFL advisor and inspector she has worked extensively with several local education authorities giving pre- and post-inspection advice and worked with staff on curriculum review and development. She was a participant in the Comenius Project entitled 'Creative Dialogues' between 2003–6 that developed Storyline as an alternative MFL teaching approach. Her research interests include MFL and connective pedagogy and overcoming barriers to pupil achievement in the subject.

Mike Calvert is Head of Continuing Professional Development at York St John University College. He lectures on research and reflective practice at a variety of levels and is an active researcher in the areas of citizenship and pastoral care. He supervises students carrying out research at undergraduate and postgraduate levels. He has been working in the area of action research since the late 80s and is keen to promote it as a vehicle for reflective practice and personal and professional development.

Gary Chambers was educated in Northern Ireland and taught German and Latin in secondary schools in Cleveland and London before joining the School of Education, University of Leeds in 1989. He completed his PhD on 'Motivational perspectives of secondary school pupils taking German' in 1996. As Senior Lecturer in Education (Modern Languages) his teaching responsibilities have included initial teacher education, higher degrees and some undergraduate work. His major research interest is motivation and foreign language learning. He is a former editor of *The Language Learning Journal*.

Sue Field is Senior Lecturer in the Faculty of Education at Canterbury Christ Church University. Following almost 20 years' experience of teaching modern foreign languages in comprehensive schools, she came to Christ Church after a period of time as head of department. Since then, she has taught and supervised students on PGCE and Masters courses, including the NQT accreditation programme, and has recently undertaken the role of Partnership Team Leader in East Kent. Sue is also on the core project team responsible for the Teacher Training Resource Bank (TTRB), a website funded by the Training and Development Agency for Schools (TDA), providing reviews of materials and resources which contribute to the research and evidence base underpinning teacher education. Currently studying for a Doctorate in Education, Sue's research interests range from teaching and learning languages to policy and practice in all areas of education.

Suzanne Graham is Subject Leader for the PGCE MFL course at the Institute of Education, University of Reading. She also works as an MFL advisor. She has taught French and German in secondary schools. Suzanne has a wide range of research interests in the field of MFL teaching and learning, including learner strategies, motivation and listening comprehension. She has given numerous papers on these topics at national and international conferences and has a wide range of publications. She supervises MA and PhD students in these areas.

Ruth Heilbronn is a Lecturer in Education at the Institute of Education, University of London where her responsibilities have included subject leader for the Secondary PGCE in MFL; team leader for PGCE Professional Studies, and module leader for the Masters of Teaching. Her research, publishing and consultancy experience and interests include the induction of newly qualified teachers; mentoring for the growth of professional knowledge and understanding, and the use of professional development portfolios in professional learning. She has wide experience of senior management in urban secondary schools, including responsibility for CPD, and she has led various MFL teams as a Head of Department and LEA adviser.

Marilyn Hunt is Lecturer in Modern Foreign Languages (Teacher Education) at the University of Warwick where she works with student teachers and MFL staff in schools on a range of teaching and learning issues. Prior to this, she was Head of Languages faculty in a comprehensive school where she taught French and Spanish. Her research interests include primary MFL teaching and assessment. She has been a member of research teams in work for SCAA, QCA and DfEE and a consultant to the Coventry LEA Languages Project 'Thinking through languages at key stage 2'. She is currently involved in two research projects with EU partners, one to develop an on-line evaluation model of language competences, related to modern foreign languages and the other to investigate ways of teaching and learning MFL in primary schools where there are no specialist MFL teachers through new technologies, for example, videoconferencing. Academic publications include chapters in books, journal articles and conference proceedings.

Shirley Lawes is Subject Leader for Modern Foreign Languages at the Institute of Education, University of London. She has considerable experience in teaching French in Secondary schools, Further Education, Adult Education and industry and for the past 12 years has worked as a PGCE tutor and researcher. Shirley is the editor of *Francophonie*, one of the language-specific journals of the Association for Language Learning and is a member of National Centre for Languages Advisory Groups on teacher training and research. Within the area of foreign languages teaching and learning, she has a particular interest in the role of culture and, in particular, the use of film in the foreign languages classroom as a cultural medium. She has published widely on a number of aspects of foreign language teaching and learning and on teacher education.

Lynne Meiring has 15 years' experience as a teacher of modern foreign languages in secondary schools. She has a Masters degree in education and has been involved in teacher education for the past 15 years (currently at Swansea School of Education). She lectures on the PGCE modern languages course and on a range of Masters degree modules including SEN, MFL and curriculum and assessment. She also supervises dissertations at Masters level. She has several publications in the field of modern language teaching. She is currently introducing a modern foreign language component into the primary PGCE course at Swansea School of Education. Lynne is also currently involved in an ESRC project looking at the impact of ICT on teaching and learning. Her particular focus is to research the impact of ICT on the learning of French in Key Stage 3 and on the learning of second language Welsh in Key Stages 1 and 2. She is also acting as a consultant to the project on SEN issues. Lynne is also a Section 10 and independent school inspector with The Office of Her Majesty's Chief Inspector of Education and Training in Wales (ESTYN) and works independently with several modern language departments on a consultancy basis.

Trevor Mutton co-ordinates and teaches on the Modern Foreign Languages PGCE at the University of Oxford, following a background as a secondary school teacher. He has also led a number of postgraduate diploma courses including those related to the professional development of modern languages teachers and to the development of teachers in the initial stages of their career. His own research work began with a focus on pupils' experiences of summative and formative assessment during their secondary school careers, but current interests are in teachers' professional development and in particular the learning of recently qualified modern languages teachers, the latter being the focus of his ongoing doctoral work.

Nigel Norman is Senior Lecturer in Education at Swansea School of Education (formerly University of Wales Swansea Department of Education), where he teaches on the PGCE Secondary MFL course, and is responsible for the Professional Studies programme. He has taught on Masters' courses and supervises Masters' dissertations. After 17 years' teaching experience in secondary schools in England and Germany he became Advisory Teacher in Wiltshire, where he was involved in curriculum development, in-service training and resources management. He has published course materials for German teaching, journal articles and reviews, and is currently Reviews Editor for *Language Learning Journal*. His research interests include the methodology of language teaching, grammar and literacy and the impact of ICT on language learning. He is currently involved in an ESRC-funded project on Interactivity and ICT, focusing on Key Stage 3 French and Key Stage 2 Welsh.

Norbert Pachler is Associate Dean: Initial and Continuing Professional Development, Deputy Head of the School of Culture, Language and Communication as well as Co-Director of the Centre for Excellence in Work based Learning for Education Professionals at the Institute of Education, University of London. Apart from the application of new technologies in teaching and learning, his research interests include computer-mediated professional teacher learning, all aspects of foreign language teaching and learning and (comparative) teacher education. He has published widely in these fields. He holds a Dr. Phil. degree, has taught in secondary and further education and has worked for the inspectorate and advisory service of a local education authority on curriculum development and in-service training. He carries out PhD/EdD supervision in the areas of teacher development, language education and ICT (with an emphasis on computer-mediated communication). Norbert has written and edited numerous books and is currently co-editor of *The Language Learning Journal* and *German as a Foreign Language*, associate editor of *The London Review of Education* and editor of *Reflecting Education*.

Ana Redondo is Lecturer in Education in the School of Culture, Language and Communication at the Institute of Education, University of London. Ana has been a Head of Modern languages and Senior Teacher for a number of years in secondary schools and has extensive experience in mentoring PGCE students from a number of ITE providers. Ana is an experienced in-service trainer for newly qualified as well as experienced teachers in a number of areas within MFL teaching and learning.

Series editors' introduction

This practical and accessible workbook is part of a series of textbooks for student teachers. It complements and extends the popular textbook entitled *Learning to Teach in the Secondary School: A Companion to School Experience*, as well as the subject-specific textbook *Learning to Teach Modern Foreign Languages in the Secondary School*. We anticipate that you will want to use this book in conjunction with these other books.

Teaching is rapidly becoming a more research- and evidence-informed profession. We have used research and professional evidence about what makes good practice to underpin the 'Learning to Teach in the Secondary School' series and these practical workbooks. Both the generic and subject-specific books in the series provide theoretical, research and professional evidence-based advice and guidance to support you as you focus on developing aspects of your teaching or your pupils' learning as you progress through your initial teacher education course and beyond. Although the generic and subject-specific books include some case studies and tasks to help you consider the issues, the practical application of material is not their major focus. That is the role of this book.

This book aims to reinforce your understanding of aspects of your teaching, support you in aspects of your development as a teacher and your teaching and enable you to analyse your success as a teacher in maximising pupils' learning by focusing on practical applications. The practical activities in this book can be used in a number of ways. Some activities are designed to be undertaken by you individually, others as a joint task in pairs and yet others as group work working with, for example, other student teachers or a school- or university-based tutor. Your tutor may use the activities with a group of student teachers. The book has been designed so that you can write directly into it.

In England, new ways of working for teachers are being developed through an initiative remodelling the school workforce. This may mean that you have a range of colleagues to support in your classroom. They also provide an additional resource on which you can draw. In any case, you will, of course, need to draw on additional resources to support your development and the *Learning to Teach in the Secondary School, 4th edition* website (www.routledge.com/textbooks/0415363926) lists key websites for Scotland, Wales, Northern Ireland and England. For example, key websites relevant to teachers in England include the Teacher Training Resource Bank (www.ttrb.ac.uk). Others include: www.teachernet.gov.uk, which is part of the DfES schools web initiative; www.becta.org.uk, which has ICT resources; and www.qca.org.uk, which is the Qualifications and Curriculum Authority website.

We do hope that this practical workbook will be useful in supporting your development as a teacher.

Susan Capel
Marilyn Leask
May 2006

Introduction

This workbook complements the successful textbook *Learning to Teach MFL in the Secondary School* by Norbert Pachler and Kit Field, also published by Routledge, and covers the practical application of a wide range of topics of direct relevance to foreign language teaching including:

- methodological approaches to foreign language teaching;
- how best to use the target language as a medium for instruction and interaction in the foreign language classroom;
- planning and assessment;
- teaching the four language skills – listening, speaking, reading and writing;
- practical approaches to the teaching of grammar, ICT and the role of cultural awareness;
- building on the foundation laid in primary schools;
- working with other adults in the classroom;
- your own professional development through teacher research.

The book brings together work by colleagues from various teacher education institutions across the country who share their wide range of expertise and experience in working with beginner teachers. The chapters illustrate good practice and provide detailed guidance on everyday pedagogical challenges; importantly, they are also grounded in key professional writing in the field.

Each chapter includes:

- an explicit statement about aims and/or objectives of the chapter;
- a detailed discussion of relevant issues and concepts;
- a series of practical tasks which allow you to apply the material presented to your own professional practice;
- a reference section listing a number of relevant background readings and websites allowing you to deepen your knowledge in each of the areas covered.

Working through the material presented in the various chapters will enable you to reach specific objectives in relation to learning to teach MFL in the secondary school by engaging with specific aspects of subject knowledge and pedagogical practice at a conceptual level as well as with practical tasks designed to enhance your learning of these aspects. In this way, the book introduces a range of tried-and-tested approaches, designed to support your development in MFL teaching.

REFERENCES

Pachler, N. and Field, K. (2001) *Learning to Teach Modern Foreign Languages in the Secondary School*. Second edition. London: RoutledgeFalmer

Part 1 Key pedagogical issues and planning

Chapter 1   Communicative approaches to modern foreign language teaching and using the target language

ANN BARNES

Chapter aims

By the end of this chapter you should:

- understand the main issues involved in communicative language teaching (CLT);
- be aware of the debate surrounding the use of the target language (TL) in the classroom;
- have gained an insight into some of the misconceptions surrounding CLT;
- have considered via some practical activities how these debates apply to MFL teaching and learning.

WHAT IS MFL TEACHING ALL ABOUT?

Whenever you read or hear about the teaching and learning of MFL, you learn that there is no definitive answer to how people learn a foreign language. There is, of course, a large body of accumulated knowledge on various factors involved in the process. This apparent lack of clarity could mean we can adapt our methodology to suit the circumstances, ourselves and the learners. However, it also means there is no ready-made recipe to follow with guaranteed results. The vast amount of advice and research available on the teaching and learning of MFL creates a multi-layered collage of bullet point lists and example activities, as well as supposed rules and recommendations, and also the various legislative requirements, official guidelines and recommended frameworks surrounding everyday teaching. Although there may be some generally agreed principles, there appear to be no cast-iron certainties; a perfectly suitable method or activity for one group of learners can fail miserably with another. Some learners feel unsure if they do not have an English equivalent immediately, others revel in trying to work out everything in the TL. A grammar 'rule' may be grasped with enthusiasm by one learner and regarded with horror by another.

MFL are also in a unique position in the school curriculum: the *medium* of 'instruction', the language in which lessons are conducted, is also the *message* of the lessons, the goal. Unlike mother-tongue or second-language teaching, where learners will encounter the 'target' throughout their day in other curriculum areas, through TV, adverts, conversations overheard on the bus, for a foreign language, as soon as the lesson is over, any language encountered is usually no longer the TL. This is, of course, the scenario painted so famously by Hawkins (1987: 99), in which he likened the teaching of MFL to 'gardening in a gale'. The weather analogy could equally be digging in a snowstorm: as soon as holes are dug, they are filled in again. However, it can also be said that learning a foreign language could be a welcome exotic encounter, a tropical island in the midst of a sea of English. As an MFL teacher, you cannot escape the facts of the situation: that French, German, Spanish or Italian is unlikely to infiltrate a great deal of your learners' lives outside your classroom (although this can be improved!), and that English is undeniably a very influential and powerful world language. But whether your classroom resembles a windswept garden devoid of its seeds or a tropical island where people would like to stay longer and learn more is to a great extent in your hands.

WHAT DO WE WANT FOREIGN LANGUAGE LEARNERS TO KNOW, UNDERSTAND AND DO?

Think about what it is you would like your learners to achieve through their MFL learning. One shared aim is probably that we would like learners to become *users* of the TL, incorporating both so-called receptive skills (listening, reading) and productive ones (speaking, writing); in short, to be able to communicate. We may also agree that they should as far as possible become *independent* in their foreign language use. If these are the aims, then MFL classes, tasks and approaches need to contribute towards these aims, to cover the necessary steps to get there. How do we expect learners to do all this? Although there is no definite answer to 'How do learners best learn a foreign language?', what is certain is that solely learning phrases 'parrot fashion' will not help them reach the above goals, nor will merely reciting grammar rules – although these activities may have a role to play in the repertoire as a whole. Learners need an approach which involves the *glue* of the language, which enables learners to generate their own language, however simple those utterances might be. In order to do this, learners need language *input* of some kind, and then they need to *do something* with that language (i.e. *output*). Learners need to understand the *why* of language learning activities as well as the *what*, so they can become increasingly independent. In order to achieve this, learners need to do much more than *encounter* bits of the language, they need to *learn* it, *investigate* it, *use* it, *own* it.

HOW DO WE EXPECT LEARNERS TO ACHIEVE ALL THIS?

Try to envisage an MFL lesson in your mind's eye. What is going on? Picture the learners and what they are doing; conjure up the sounds that might be heard; imagine the teacher and the teacher's behaviour. Think about what the pupils might be able to see or refer to. The scene which emerges in your imagination may be very different from that which is conjured up in mine and that of other MFL teachers. What is perfectly 'normal' for one MFL teacher (for example, pupils working individually on language exercises) may be alien to another, who prefers a substantial amount of collaborative learning. Additionally, what may occur in the lesson one day may contrast with the activity experienced by the same class with the same teacher on another day, or even in the previous five minutes. There will be a vast number of different imagined scenarios, a vast number of scenarios occur in MFL lessons; the manifestation of the 'how' of foreign language learning. Despite this variety, for many years the MFL community as a whole, certainly in the UK, has tended to claim subscription to communicative language teaching (CLT). *Communication* in the TL, in order to *learn* to communicate in the TL: the medium of learning and the message are combined.

WHAT IS MEANT BY CLT?

CLT has been described and explored extensively in the last decades (see Chapter 3 in *Learning to Teach MFL in the Secondary School*, second edition, Routledge, for a detailed overview). An 'approach', implying guidance rather than rules, is clearly different to a 'method', which implies a substantial degree of prescription. CLT revolves around a number of principles, rather than a list of edicts, and takes into account the individual learners and

Activity 1.1

Look at the verbs below. They could all conceivably be used in lesson plans to show what the pupils and you will be doing.

collaborate	listen	imagine	use
act out	practise	introduce	manipulate
revise	highlight	describe	predict
outline	connect	guess	learn
exemplify	create	demonstrate	chant
list	order	challenge	choose
model	enunciate	copy	read
elicit	deduce	repeat	spot
prioritise	memorise	think	summarise
decide			

- What pupil learning and thinking is implied with each verb?
- In lessons you have observed or taught, how many of these verbs could have been used to describe what pupils were doing?
- Which other verbs have you seen exemplified in MFL classrooms?
- Are there any you would like to add which you have not encountered in practice?

the particular context. Because it is an 'approach', it can seem a little intangible; there is no definitive protocol for foreign language learning and teaching and it is, perhaps, therefore more open to misinterpretation or partial understanding than a method. Sato and Kleinsasser (1999: 501) found that although the teachers they studied *claimed* to follow a broadly CLT approach, they were able only to provide fragmentary, and varied, explanations of what that entailed. In a UK context, Block (2002: 23) found a similar partial understanding of CLT amongst MFL teachers. Common misconceptions about CLT include exclusive use of the TL, an almost wholly oral approach and neglect of grammar and structure where fluency is always prioritised over accuracy. Any investigation into the full implications of CLT contradicts these misconceptions and reveals, for example, that grammar is part of true communicative teaching (see Pachler, 2000) and that CLT, properly implemented, does *not* exclude the use of L1, despite this being a widely held view (see, for example, Macaro, 2001).

CLT is an approach which seeks to enable learners to progress in their foreign language learning. The essential question is: what do the learners need to learn and how best will they achieve this? CLT involves a balance of linguistic form and function, grammar and communication (see Figure 1.1). Neither should dominate, although either may take priority at certain points in the learning process. None of the principles of CLT include learning language forms for their own sake, devoid of context and purpose. However, neither do these principles *ignore* language forms: the grammar of the language is an intrinsic part of CLT. It is important for learners to be able to manipulate the forms in order to communicate; it is also important for them to be able to express themselves without being held

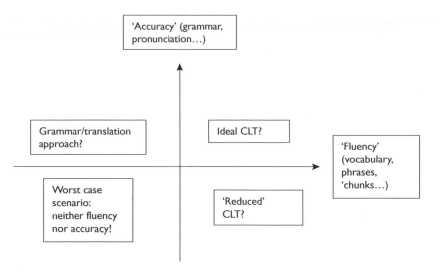

Figure 1.1 What do the learners need to learn and how best will they achieve this?

back by over-focusing on form. What they need most will vary at different times for different learners.

DOES EVERYTHING HAVE TO BE COMMUNICATIVE?

Learning a language through communication may seem a blindingly obvious concept – after all, what is the aim of foreign language teaching, if not successful communication, the imparting and receiving of information? But there is a process required before learners can communicate fully. They need to receive language input, practise this language for themselves and then *use* the language in a communicative way. However, this process, albeit at a very basic level, may happen very quickly. For example, learners could be introduced to ten vocabulary items via the use of visuals. These items could be something very straightforward such as pictures of animals.

Activity 1.2

The sequence below outlines what is probably a familiar pattern to you from lessons you have observed or taught.

- In your chosen TL, expand stages 1–6 below by supplying the relevant vocabulary and activities as appropriate, taking care to consider such issues as gender of nouns, familiarity of cognates and relative ease/difficulty of pronunciation/spelling.
- Reflect on the *purpose* of each step. What specifically are learners doing, thinking about, learning at each stage?
- Which of the stages, in your opinion, involve true *communication*?

1   Learners hear ten items presented in a logical sequence with visuals (input).

_____

_____

Activity 1.2 *continued*

2   They may, almost simultaneously, see the written forms (input).

_____

_____

3   They understand the meanings (opportunity for assessment).

_____

_____

4   They repeat the items sufficient times to feel confident with the pronunciation (opportunity for assessment).

_____

_____

5   They practise these items through a variety of activities, involving more demanding cognitive processes where possible (opportunity for assessment).

_____

_____

6   They use them to communicate a message (perhaps a true personal message, perhaps hypothetical) (opportunity for assessment).

_____

_____

Not all the stages involve communication in its full sense. Some activities are *pre-communicative* (see Littlewood, 1981); for example, when repeating lexical items, the purpose of the activity is *not* to communicate meaning, but to practise pronunciation and begin to memorise and 'own' the vocabulary. These are crucial steps in learning the language; communicative activities only succeed when the pre-communicative stages of comprehensively presenting the language that will be required and practising it intensively are completed. Pre-communicative activities can (and should!) be fun and cognitively demanding. There is absolutely nothing wrong with this in a classroom where teaching and learning are taking place, as long as there is purpose and the activities lead somewhere; to learn a language by true communication alone would usually involve immersion in the TL culture. If learning never or only rarely progresses beyond the pre-communicative, then learners will not achieve any real success. If all elements of communication are eliminated, then the learning will not be as effective and the activities will become dry and unstimulating. In order to communicate, learners need to progress through pre-communicative stages, but as soon as possible an element of communication should be introduced for effective learning to take place. For example, in the sequence outlined in Activity 1.2, a simple 'hide the visual' activity can provoke real communication. Pointing at a visual and asking the learners 'What is this?' is repetition, and valid at an early stage (perhaps to enable the teacher to assess which linguistic items need to be modelled again), but it is not *communication*. Secretly hiding one visual and asking the learners which one they think is hidden is much more akin to true communication (and produces more language). Similarly, asking learners personal questions involving the new vocabulary, such as 'What pets do you have?', is also communicative as you, the teacher, as well as other learners, do not (necessarily) know the answer.

In order to create 'communication' in the classroom, CLT espoused the information gap activity, where Pupil A has some information which pupil B does not have. B must get this information successfully to complete the task. It can be that both pupil A and pupil B have some of the missing information. A simple information gap is asking someone which they prefer out of a list of hobbies for example. 'What is your name, Lisa?' is certainly not an information gap!

Activity 1.3

'Pre-communicative activities focus on linguistic structures or vocabulary items. Communicative activities require learners to put into use the structures and vocabulary they have been practising for communication' (Morgan and Neil, 2001: 7).

Are the activities below pre-communicative or communicative? Or could they be both?

1   Practising a dialogue acting out various emotions
2   Imitation
3   Pair work
4   Conversation cue cards with symbols
5   Group work
6   Surveys
7   Listening comprehension
8   Deciding which restaurant is the best
9   Role play
10 Identifying/extracting written information
11 Interviews
12 Recognising new language
13 True/false activity
14 Learning by heart
15 Language games
16 Listening for gist/detail
17 Expressing opinions
18 Planning/carrying out group activities
19 Producing creative texts
20 Choosing a holiday from a brochure
21 Describing the ideal holiday
22 Matching up boyfriends/girlfriends from clues

THE UNIQUE NATURE OF THE MFL CLASSROOM:
THE MEDIUM IS THE MESSAGE

The use of the TL within CLT has been perhaps over-interpreted. The MFL classroom, particularly in the UK, is in a strange position. For a short period of time, say 45 minutes for three times a week, learners, if they are lucky, encounter a TL experience, which they have to accept, interpret, absorb, deal with and learn from. They then probably will not hear, read, speak or write this language until the next lesson, except perhaps for some homework. This argument has been used for many years and remains valid. The *quality* of the TL brief encounters, therefore, needs to be very high, very clear and very consistent. It is a missed opportunity to expose learners to more TL input for example if something very straightforward is transmitted in L1. Similarly, if unstructured TL use results in pupils' incomprehension and demotivation, then it is also wasted. Learners must feel a sense of confidence, curiosity and achievement in MFL – a subject where skills, knowledge and understanding are acquired cumulatively and not in a straightforward, linear manner. Individual items of vocabulary can be learnt discretely and without recourse to previous learning, but if the fundamentals of the language, the elements which enable production, are lost, then learners will feel powerless. Foreign language learners need to achieve success in very short bursts in far from ideal circumstances.

Activity 1.4

Looking at activities is best done in threes if possible, where two people complete the activity and one observes.

- Select some pupil activities from a unit of work/coursebook.
- 'Do' the activity.
- Think about each activity's:

  - clarity of instructions/procedure
  - purpose
  - position in a learning sequence (practice? drill? production? genuine communication?)
  - *need* to use the TL.

- What would the pupils have to know/understand/be able to do before tackling the activity?
- Is the emphasis in the activity on form or function or both?

When learners are confused or misled by the use of the TL it is obviously counter-productive. At the extreme are classrooms where teacher TL predominates, but where pupils do not understand enough about *how* the TL works to generate any themselves, or are overwhelmed by a torrent of incomprehensible TL (see Chapter 5 in *Learning to Teach MFL in the Secondary School*, second edition, Routledge, for a detailed discussion of this issue). Learners need to be able to build their language up confidently. Often, the vast majority of a lesson will be conducted in the TL (and the pupils will use a lot of TL themselves); on other occasions, a considerable amount of English may be used legitimately; for example, to discuss and debate language learning strategies. Learners do not need to hear *you* using the TL to be impressed; they need to hear and see *themselves* understanding and using the TL to be motivated by their own progress. Watching expert acrobats does not lead to the audience performing somersaults, even if they might be able to recognise one.

If learners are exposed to 100% unstructured TL, they may learn a little.

If learners are exposed to 100% structured TL, they should learn some.

If learners are exposed to optimal, structured TL, with rationalised use of L1 they should learn most effectively.

(Macaro, 2000)

If you can get pupils to see *why* using the TL helps them progress in their foreign language learning, this is excellent. Your TL use may differ from class to class – this is not a problem, as long as the learners are progressing in their foreign language. The first question to ask yourself at the end of a lesson or series of lessons is: 'Did the pupils learn and make progress?' Your usage of the TL will inevitably be part of this – after all, there is a very limited time for them to learn a foreign language, so the more exposure they have to the language the better, but this exposure has to be understood and absorbed for them to make any real progress at all beyond mimicry. Enabling the learners to use the TL appropriately is also crucial here: you may ask a question which they fully understand, but because they feel unsure as to how to answer correctly, they may say nothing at all. They require frameworks to help them get there and need to feel secure in your classroom and with the TL. Meiring and Norman (2002) argued for establishing a pedagogic rationale for using TL. *Planning* when and why L1 is used in your classroom is vital. A lesson with almost 100 per cent TL may still not be as productive as one with 70 or 80 per cent, where pupils generate and manipulate the language themselves.

SUMMARY

The chapters in this book exemplify effective, communicative approaches to MFL teaching and learning. This chapter has introduced you to some of the main issues involved in this. Adopting truly communicative language teaching involves planning and teaching to enable learners, as far as possible, to communicate in the TL and become independent in their language learning.

USEFUL WEBSITES

www.llas.ac.uk/index.aspx the Subject Centre for Languages, Linguistics and Area Studies, has a large number of 'Good Practice' articles available electronically, which, whilst aimed primarily at higher education, offer some interesting perspectives on foreign language teaching and learning.

www.scilt.stir.ac.uk/SLR/ the Scottish Languages Review is an electronic journal which offers a variety of articles on a wide range of aspects of foreign language teaching and learning.

www.ALL-languages.org.uk the website of the Association for Language Learning, which provides up-to-date information on the situation of foreign languages in the curriculum and useful links.

www.cilt.org.uk the website of CILT, the National Centre for Languages, which again has a wide range of links and information.

Chapter 2   Planning modern foreign language lessons

RUTH HEILBRONN

Chapter aims

By the end of this chapter you should:

- understand some basic principles of modern foreign language (MFL) planning;
- understand the role of evaluation in good planning;
- start planning individual lessons.

STARTING OFF

In planning lessons, much depends on the context of your work, including your teaching style, your students and the school. There is no individual template for MFL planning but there are fundamental principles. These are based on research findings on how a second MFL is acquired/learnt.

There is no short cut to good planning but if done well, your students are helped to learn effectively and this feeds back into your sense of confidence and achievement. Below are suggestions to help planning, but first some fundamentals to consider:

1   *An individual lessons fits into a longer term plan.* This may be an examination syllabus or a scheme of work (SoW) covering an academic year. The head of department, or a team of teachers produces the SoW, which may be taken from a textbook scheme.
2   *Students are your primary focus.* What should they learn and how can they best learn it? You need to know the students individually in order to plan their learning.
3   *Evaluation is essential.* How do you find out how well the students have learnt what you taught them?

Therefore:

1   *Focus on the students and the previous lessons.* What happened in recent lessons? What have they covered on the SoW, or textbook or syllabus and what still needs to be done?
2   *What is the context for the lesson?* Is it first thing in the morning or last lesson on Friday afternoon? When will the students need settling and when 'stirring' or stimulating?
3   *'Frame' the lesson.* Identify specifically and precisely what you intend to teach.

Activity 2.1

1 Read the suggestions below for framing precise teaching and learning objectives for each lesson (A).
2 Read the example text (B).
3 Formulate some objectives of your own (C).

(A) Examples of possible objectives

* *Present*

    – ten new items of vocabulary using the indefinite article;
    – the third person present of the verb tener;
    – me gusta(n); changing a statement into a question.

* *Consolidate* singular and plural nouns: *un hermano/una hermana/dos hermanos/tres hermanas.*
* *Revise* expressions for the weather: *il fait/il y a*; question words.
* *Recycle* days of the week, times, school subjects.
* *Explain* the abbreviations used in the dictionary.
* *Introduce* the Spanish-speaking world.
* *Model* ideas for memorising vocabulary.

(B) An example linguistic objective

Students will learn to describe the things in their bedroom. They will revise the structure '*Hay*' and practise the two structures '*En mi dormitoria hay . . .*' with various items of vocabulary.

(C) Write objectives for a lesson

Check the following: Are they specific enough as in the example? Will they enable you to build specific lesson activities?

_____

_____

NEXT STEPS

1 *Contextualise the objectives* for your students. What can you incorporate from their experience to draw them towards the material? Examples are using flashcards of the Simpsons for introducing family vocabulary, or contrasting Homer Simpson with a sports personality when teaching the negative. For example, in French: '*Thierry Henry fait du sport. Homer ne fait pas de sport*'.

2 *Think how to make the objective accessible to all.* This means having precise information on each individual pupil relating to his or her prior attainment. Do some individuals achieve consistently above the average of the rest of the class? Do any have any defined special needs? Access information, such as reports from previous teachers, and make observations based on specific educational outcomes, such how pupils answer questions in class, work in their exercise books, or work together in groups. Information

about pupils' prior learning achievements should be available and you should record an individual profile of each pupil. Figure 2.1 shows part of a Year 7 class record with some of the available information. It is easy to see at a glance that Pupil A will need some form of extension in the lesson, Pupil C needs to be watched for production of homework and Pupil B needs to be supported with clear instructions and possibly extra steps in some exercises.

Name	Extension Needed or Gifted / Talented	EAL Level	Reading Age	Target for HW
Pupil A	Yes	–	14	–
Pupil B		2	8	–
Pupil C	Yes	–	13	Yes

Figure 2.1 Example of a recording format page

3   *Identify and formulate the learning outcomes* by deciding exactly what the students will be able to do at the end of the lesson that they could not do at the beginning. Work out more than one possible level of attainment, using your knowledge about the students and your judgement about what is achievable. It is useful to think in terms of *must, should* and *could*: what everyone *must* be able to do at the end of the lesson; what most *should* do, in addition to the basic tasks; and if you need a level of extension above that, a few pupils *could* do extra. In strictly set classes, two levels only may be sufficient and practicable.

Activity 2.2

1   Read the suggestions below for framing the learning outcomes for pupils (A).
2   Read the example text (B).
3   Formulate some statements of your own (C).

(A) Some possible learning outcomes

By the end of the lesson:

- *all pupils* will be able to:

  - *recognise* the new nouns when they see or hear them and pronounce them with confidence *after a model*; understand n.m/n.f when they look up a noun in the dictionary;
  - *have a record* of which countries in the world speak Spanish.

- *most pupils* will be able to write sentences using the past tense *with the help of the prompt sheet*.
- *some pupils* will be able to *create* their own questions orally *without support*.

Activity 2.2 *continued*

(B) Example text

All students will understand information containing the structure and vocabulary when heard and read and make a relevant oral statement containing the structure.
Most students will also add colour descriptions or other adjectives orally.
Some students will be able to extend this to produce longer sentences and express opinions both orally and in writing.

(C) Write some outcomes for the objective you planned in Activity 2.1

Check if realistic and achievable – how will you tell if they are?

_____

_____

PLANNING THE ACTIVITIES

When you have formulated the teaching and learning objectives and the outcomes you expect from the students, you have a frame within which to plan the activities of the lesson. Here, too, there are points for reflection:

1 *Think about the lesson from the students' point of view*
   How active will they be, how engaged and actively participating? Students need a great deal of practice to enable them to commit new material to their long-term memory. Build in activities for them to practise and consolidate at each phase of the lesson. In the planning pro forma in Figure 2.2 for example, there is space to mark what both the teacher and the pupil will do in each activity, and the time it will take. You need to be able to think of the lesson in advance from both these perspectives.

2 *Planning the activities*
   When planning the activities it is helpful to think of the skills of Listening and Speaking as one phase and Reading and Writing as a second phase. Later chapters will refine this notion relating to the skills to cover. At this stage, think broadly in terms of enabling pupils to have enough oral practice of what has been introduced aurally to them. Likewise, enable them to have enough reading practice of what they have heard and said. Design the activities with the learning outcomes in mind. Does the activity further your aim of getting the pupils to achieve their learning outcomes at the end of the lesson? They need to be actively involved in their learning, through motivating and interesting activities. Here good resources are essential.

3 *How will you judge if your lesson is successful?*
   Be clear before the lesson begins how you will evaluate pupil learning. Which activities will reveal whether pupils have learnt what you have tried to teach them? If there are no opportunities for them to show what they have learnt, you will not be able to tell how effective the lesson has been. As the lesson progresses, you will be able to pick up on feedback from the pupils. This can come from various sources, such marking individual pupils' work. In class you could choose a pupil who represents a number of others in achievement, as a gauge for their sample group. Asking targeted questions to about four or five judiciously chosen pupils can give you a lot of information about the whole-class

achievement, providing you know the class well. Assessing how pupils are learning requires teachers to be alert to the learners' progress so as to make adjustments to the ongoing classroom situation.

Activity 2.3

Read the suggestions below for gaining information on students' learning in the lesson. Then refer back to your reflections on Activities 2.1 and 2.2 to formulate some assessment opportunities.

- *Typical assessment opportunities in the activities are*:

  Any activities requiring application of taught content – for example a gapfill activity;

  an explanation about why a particular verb ending is used;

  a role-play activity demonstrating retention and production of language;

  oral and written answers to questions.

- Possibilities for checking on learning, such as:

  Listening and Reading – *whole-class marking and monitoring during a listening exercise*.

  Spoken – *during presentation; individually directed question and answers, and individual monitoring during pairwork*.

  Written – *take books in and mark*.

- *Formulate some assessment opportunities* (refer back to your answers on Activities 2.1. and 2.2.).

  _____

  _____

  _____

- *Check that assessment opportunities* are realistic, manageable, achievable. Will they give you the kind of information you need to check if they have achieved the objective of the lesson?

Activity 2.4

Using the planning pro forma in Figure 2.2, plan a whole lesson based on the activities in this chapter.

  Schools may use different formats but using the pro forma suggested has the advantage of allowing you to think through all the stages described here and to record your thinking systematically.

Activity 2.4

Class:	Time:	Date:	Language:

Teaching and learning objectives:

Learning Outcomes	Assessment Opportunities
Core level 1 SEN & EAL **All** students will be able to:	
Core Level 2: **Most students** will be able to	
Extension: **Some** students will be able to	

AT Levels – Range covered: (This refers to the Attainment Targets of the National Curriculum)

Previous learning outcomes
(Here add what pupils have already covered)

Lesson __ out of __
(Here add how many lessons on the topic or area have been covered)

Activity 2.4 *continued*

Timing	Activities (This section can be extended to cover all the activities planned for the lesson)		PoS
Time	Activities – plenaries marked *		PoS
	Teacher	Pupils	

Activity 2.4 *continued*

Resources required

ICT

Homework

Evaluation

Pupil learning. Were the learning outcomes achieved?	Own teaching

Action to be taken for next lesson – arising from evaluation and feedback

Figure 2.2 Planning pro forma

EVALUATING THE LESSON

After the lesson is over you need to evaluate it in order to plan the next lesson. Reflect on what happened in terms of:

1   *Pupil learning*. Did the pupils achieve the learning outcomes? You may need to wait until you have marked exercise books, although you should have evidence from sources such as targeted questioning in whole-class work.
2   *Own teaching*. Was what you planned and executed the best way to achieve your ends?
3   *Implications for future lessons*. What will you do next? If something has not been fully or properly understood, it will need to be tackled again or the pupils will have an insecure basis for moving on.

There are some useful prompts for your evaluation in Activity 2.5. You should select specific questions relevant to the particular lesson at the end of each lesson. Your notes can be brief but should lead to future planning.

Activity 2.6 will help you begin to engage with medium-term planning for each of your classes at the beginning of the teaching period.

Activity 2.5

1   Use the following guide and reflect on a lesson you have taught. Choose three questions and answer them.
2   Repeat with another lesson and different questions.
3   What is the aim of lesson evaluation? Do you think it is important?

Guide to evaluation

Pupil learning

1   Were the learning objectives clear to me?
2   Were the learning outcomes clear to me?
3   Did the pupils achieve the learning outcomes? How do I know this?
4   Did pupils know what they were trying to achieve in each of the activities and parts of the lesson?

Own teaching

1   Were my instructions clear?
2   Did I use the target language appropriately?
3   Did I include pair/group work?
4   Were there opportunities for independent learning?
5   Did I cover all four skills?
6   Did I make good use of resources?
7   How did I cover cultural awareness?
8   Did the order and structure of the lesson work for the pupils' benefit? Do I need to rethink this?

Activity 2.5 *continued*

Differentiation

1 Were the material and lesson content appropriate for the group?
2 Do I know what individual pupils' strengths and weaknesses are?
3 Do I know all the pupils' names?
4 Did I cater for inclusion, that is, for the range of achievement in the group? How?
5 Did everyone get the opportunity to participate?
6 Did I diagnose and assess pupils' difficulties? Did I respond to them?
7 Did I include everyone by helping the more reluctant and lower achievers to join in?

General classroom management

1 Did I cope effectively with disruptions?
2 Did I ensure that everyone was on task consistently and monitor their work?
3 Pupil motivation and involvement – were pupils alert, confident, enthusiastic or apathetic, uncertain, obstructive?
4 Did I comment on work, praising effort, achievement and accuracy and give encouragement?
5 Did I and the pupils enjoy the lesson?

Activity 2.6

Take:

- the school calendar;
- your own timetable;
- current monthly or yearly planner blank format;
- SoW or exam specifications.

Work in half-term blocks. Make sure you are clear on all the term and holiday dates. Compare your timetable with the school calendar and block out any events which will take lessons away from you (such as exams, school trips). Then calculate how many lessons you will have with each of your classes. Using the SoW, plan how many lessons each unit or block of work can be allocated to the time available.

SUMMARY

At first all new teachers find the planning and evaluation as described in this chapter a laborious process, but as experience and professional judgement develop, planning lessons usually becomes much more familiar and greatly helps teachers to manage classes and workloads and to achieve good learning outcomes for students.

FURTHER READING

Deane, M. (2002) 'Planning MFL learning', in A. Swarbrick (ed) *Aspects of Teaching Secondary Modern Foreign Languages*. London and New York: RoutledgeFalmer and Open University, pp. 147–66.

Hurren, C. (1992) *Department Planning and Schemes of Work*. London: CILT.

Pachler, N. and Field, K. (2001) 'Observing, planning and evaluating Modern Foreign Language lessons', in N. Pachler and K. Field (eds) *Learning to Teach Modern Foreign Languages in the Secondary School*. Second edition. London: Routledge, pp. 62–83, 311–13.

Chapter 3   Presenting new vocabulary and structures

SUE FIELD

Chapter aims

By the end of this chapter you should:

- recognise the need to teach new vocabulary/structures;
- have an appreciation of the process of selecting key lexical items to stimulate topic-based foreign language learning;
- be aware of the range of resources available, particularly visual aids;
- be able to draw on a bank of foreign language presentation activities to sequence and structure the learning experience.

KNOWLEDGE UNDERPINNING THE TEACHING OF NEW VOCABULARY AND STRUCTURES

Assimilating vocabulary/structures is an essential part of language learning. Meaning cannot be conveyed without vocabulary. 'Words' is the first strand within the Key Stage 3 MFL Framework. Examination specifications demand that pupils acquire a vocabulary of up to 2,000 words, as well as structures and collocations (i.e. words which 'belong together', e.g. *Sport treiben*). Some vocabulary is for passive use, but the majority is for active. At A/AS level, there is no defined list of lexical items; the range of vocabulary is vast.

Vocabulary can be defined as single words, easily translatable from one language to another. Cognates (words which can transfer between languages, e.g. *radio*) present little challenge for learners. Some words contain clues to meaning, such as compound nouns and separable verbs in German, or have common stems (e.g. *verdier*). Structures, e.g. *ich möchte*, carry meaning or purpose, providing utterances with a force (requests, negatives, questions, imperatives, etc.). Concepts, consisting of combinations of words, are not directly translatable, often requiring an appreciation of cultural contexts for a full understanding.

Although vocabulary/structures are acquired incidentally throughout learning, this chapter looks at ways in which the teacher overtly facilitates the process of vocabulary learning. 'Presentation–Practice–Production' (PPP) is traditional within communicative language teaching (see e.g. *Learning to Teach MFL in the Secondary School*, second edition, Routledge, Chapter 3). It demands that, within individual lessons and throughout a series of lessons, pupils:

1   are presented sets of language forms;
2   are given opportunities to practise;
3   manipulate language for their own purposes.

The presentation stage is not only significant in terms of its position in the sequence (i.e. to engage pupils' interest from the start of the lesson), but also provides essential elements enabling pupils to participate in subsequent activities and meet specified learning outcomes.

First, learners recognise the sight and sound of the word, identified by Grauberg (1997) as 'discrimination', before moving on to 'understanding meaning'. If pupils relate the word/structure to a concept, rather than to a translation, they begin to commit this to long-term memory by connecting this to a (mental) image, sound, movement, event or process. Pupils' preferred learning styles will determine the efficacy of each of these for themselves; the first three would appeal respectively to visual, auditory and kinaesthetic learners.

WHICH VOCABULARY AND STRUCTURES, AND HOW MANY FOR EACH LESSON?

Decisions will be based upon the scheme of work, which normally relates to a textbook, examination specifications, the MFL KS3 Framework, QCA schemes of work, etc. The teacher exercises professional judgement in selecting the most useful lexical items.

Context

What are the lexical items required for this particular topic/unit, and how can this vocabulary be broken down into individual lessons?

For example, within a unit on 'Around town', directions and types of shops may be presented in separate lessons, and then learnt in combination. Key words could be *links, rechts, geradeaus*; a key structure could be *Nimm die erste Strasse . . .*

Intended learning outcomes

What should pupils be able to do with the vocabulary by the end of the lesson, and why?

Teachers must clarify whether the language is for receptive or productive use. This helps the teacher to identify key structures; for example, imperatives, questions and negatives.

Prior learning

What have pupils already learnt?

Activities enabling pupils to recall known vocabulary/structures, and to build upon them, must be considered.

Complexity of lexical items or concepts

Are these hard or easy to understand or pronounce? How many words can pupils be expected to learn, and which are for receptive or productive use?

Pupil characteristics

What is the ability range and motivation of the class? Are they beginner, intermediate or advanced learners?

Time

When does the lesson take place? How long is the lesson? These influence pupil motivation, and the quantity of new language pupils will be able to assimilate.

Activity 3.1

Choose one unit from the QCA scheme of work for KS3 French, German or Spanish (www.standards.dfes.gov.uk/schemes2) to work with for these tasks.

(A)   From reading *all* the information given within the unit of work, devise a list of vocabulary and structures which would be appropriate. Identify which are for receptive and which are for productive use. (The units are, broadly speaking, sequential, so Units 1–6 are intended for Year 7, and so on.)

Vocabulary and structures	
Productive	Receptive

Activity 3.1 *continued*

(B) Extract the pupil learning outcomes from the unit. Consider how these lexical items contribute to each of these. Divide the list of vocabulary and structures into categories appropriate for each of the learning outcomes. Within each of these categories, grade the lexical items from simple to complex.

Pupil learning outcomes	Vocabulary and structures (from simple to complex)
	– – –
	– – –
	– – –
	– – –
	– – –
	– – –

Activity 3.1 *continued*

(C) Consider how these learning outcomes might be broken down further, and re-combined into intended learning outcomes for individual lessons. Sequence these into ten lessons of one hour's duration for a class of average ability. What new lexical items would be presented in each lesson? How might you alter this for a class of low or high ability? (Consider the differentiated 'Expectations' outlined for the unit.)

	Pupil Learning Outcomes	**Vocabulary and structures**
Lesson 1	– –	
Differentiation		
Lesson 2	– –	
Differentiation		
Lesson 3	– –	
Differentiation		
Lesson 4	– –	
Differentiation		
Lesson 5	– –	
Differentiation		
Lesson 6	– –	
Differentiation		
Lesson 7	– –	
Differentiation		
Lesson 8	– –	
Differentiation		
Lesson 9	– –	
Differentiation		
Lesson 10	– –	
Differentiation		

WHICH RESOURCES TO USE?

Choosing resources for presenting language is important. For learners at Key Stages 4 and 5, this may take the form of a text (spoken or written), from which pupils extrapolate new lexical items. Tapes, CDs and a variety of reading materials serve as resources here.

For all pupils, visual aids provide an effective way to focus and engage interest, and to establish concepts. In this way, the status of the target language is enhanced at a crucial stage of the learning process. Visual aids are not only used to represent items at face value (e.g. nouns), but also to represent qualities (e.g. adjectives), as well as to symbolise longer structures (e.g. *Il n'y a pas de quoi*). Such structures (and, therefore, the same visual aids) may be used in different units, allowing for the transferability of knowledge and skills.

In choosing the visual aids, important questions are:

- Are they appropriate for the particular topic?
- Do they enable learners to use language in a quasi-authentic way?
- Will they 'grab' pupils' attention? Are they attractive, not outdated, of interest?
- Will they encourage pupils to link meaning and concept?
- How flexible are they, can they be used in subsequent activities and units?
- Is the time required to prepare them well spent?

A range of resources is available to teachers, which enables the accommodation of all learning styles over a period of time.

Flashcards	Very versatile, can be handled by pupils
OHP	Used to project pictures, words, symbols, silhouettes of objects on to a screen. On/off switch and focus button can be used to good effect. Possibility of presenting images in reverse.
Interactive whiteboard	Has all the advantages of a computer screen on display to all pupils, with the added advantages of touch-screen facilities.
Powerpoint	Can be used as 'virtual flashcards' (which can also be printed off for further use). Animation enables sound and movement to be added, as well as overlaying words. Composite pictures can be produced.
Video/CD-Rom/DVD	Combines sound (commentary) and moving image; can be 'frozen' to provide still visuals.
Visualisers	A multi-media system which combines many of the above. It has the added advantage of projecting actual items onto a screen, rather than as silhouettes.
Display (including labels)	Links concepts and images through forms of labelling. This encourages passive learning of vocabulary, as well as developing cultural awareness.
Human resources	Voice, mime, movement, expressions, gestures, obeying commands (imperatives). These add an authentic human touch. Also personal attributes, clothes, etc. – but needs sensitive handling.
Realia	Authentic items from the country where the target language is spoken. Provide opportunities for developing cultural awareness. Realia can be used and handled in an authentic way.
Props	Cross-cultural artefacts. Can be handled by the pupils.
Whiteboard	Replacement screen display area for combining written words and symbols, enabling the teacher to interact with pupils. Good for visual representation of a time-line, for tenses.

Figure 3.1 Resources for presenting language

Activity 3.2

Using the outcomes of Activity 3.1, the aim of this activity is to match appropriate resources to the new lexical items to be taught and learnt.

(A)   Consider which of the resources identified within the chapter would be most effective in presenting the particular lexical items. The teacher needs to be aware of the 'force' of the new structures (requests, negatives, questions, imperatives, etc.) in order to match this with appropriate resources.

Vocabulary and structures	Language force	Resource

(B)   Comment on the qualities of the particular resources you have identified, with reference to the list of important questions when choosing visual aids.

	Resource 1	Resource 2	Resource 3
Appropriateness to topic?			
Quasi-authenticity?			
Attention 'grabbing'?			
Conceptual linking?			
Flexibility?			
Preparation worthwhile?			

Activity 3.2 *continued*

(C)   Do the activities you have identified reflect a bias towards one particular learning style; for example visual or auditory learners? What do you need to do to balance this in your teaching? Discuss with your mentor the type of activities and resources she uses for particular topics. Can you think of ways to broaden your repertoire?

For further information see www.funderstanding.com

WHICH ACTIVITIES CAN BE INCLUDED IN THE PRESENTATION PHASE?

Harris and Snow (2004) suggest one must hear a word 12 times before it can be remembered, and, therefore, repeated exposure is required. This process relies on teacher input, although pupils must be given opportunities to use the language meaningfully, through multi-sensory activities. These need to be sequenced, allowing pupils to gain confidence. Attention should be paid to pace and transitions.

Phased activities include the following.

Listening activities

Pupils listen attentively, whilst given the opportunity to internalise new sounds.

- *Guessing what new words might be*
  Provide a stimulus for active listening; for example, a picture on the board. Items for use could be revealed slowly, providing clues to the topic area, such as clothes in a suitcase. The keyhole technique with OHP (a hole cut out of a piece of paper, moved across the transparency), or with the interactive whiteboard, can be used in the same way.

- *Identifying new words within a text*
  Circling new or key vocabulary within a text, either from a written or spoken stimulus.

- *Odd one out*
  For aural acuity purposes; pupils pick from three utterances (e.g. *les yeux verts, les yeux gris, les yeux verts*).

Listening and repeating activities

Pupils need to be encouraged to repeat after a model, practising pronunciation of new vocabulary/structures – as a whole class, as smaller groups and, finally, individually. Large groups of pupils can be resistant to choral repetition exercises, so imaginative ways to encourage pupils to take part should be deployed:

- vary the tone and style of voice;
- introduce an element of competition (one side of the room versus the other);
- hum, chant or clap to a rhythm (e.g. rap);
- build up phrases backwards (this is particularly useful as a way of building up to longer structures);
- repeat if it's true (see Buckby, 1980).

For 'repeat if it's true', pupils repeat a word or phrase only if it corresponds to the visual aid being presented at the time. Conducted as a game, it enables pupils to demonstrate what they have remembered from the initial presentation in a non-threatening climate. This moves pupils towards linking sound and image to meaning. Teachers can monitor progress on a whole-class basis, and it also encourages pupils to listen actively to new vocabulary.

Matching activities

Pupils can demonstrate on an individual basis whether or not they are making the required links to meaning. They may not generate language themselves, but they must make choices based on whether the sound and image match.

- *Pupils match images to words*
  Touching or pointing at a visual aid, or by referring to a number or name.

- *Miming, including pantomime competitions*
  Individuals or groups of pupils mime a word or action, either in response to a stimulus, or for others to speculate as to the meaning.

Question-and-answer activities

Questioning needs to be graded in order to build pupils' confidence and follow the 'hierarchy of questions':

1 *Closed questions*, requiring yes/no or true/false responses demand receptive knowledge of the language (similar to matching activities).
2 *Alternative questions* require pupils to choose between two utterances and to reproduce this language. Although a closed question, it has the benefit of allowing pupils to repeat after a model.
3 *Target or goal questions* are open, and correct answers reveal a productive knowledge of new vocabulary/structures, and a readiness to move on to the practice stage.

- *Noughts and crosses*
  The OHP or nine flashcards stuck onto the whiteboard (3×3) can be used for this. Pupils nominate a particular space on the grid for their team by correctly identifying the image within it (i.e. by providing the answer to the target question). (As pupils have a choice of up to nine utterances, they can 'get away with' not yet knowing the full list of new lexical items; see also guessing activities below.)

Guessing games

There is a range of activities which require pupils to make guesses as to the 'identity' of an item of vocabulary. This is a way of getting the pupils to produce language for themselves; it allows pupils to offer answers to open questions, even if they are not sure of the entire list of new vocabulary. Again, getting a 'wrong' answer is not threatening; it simply demonstrates they have guessed incorrectly. It provides a chance for the teacher to monitor individual pupils' progress.

- *Blind man's bluff*
  Individual pupils close their eyes, and are asked to point at images (most probably flashcards/posters) located around the room. When used for places in a town, this allows for authentic interaction (e.g. *'Où est la gare?'*, *'La gare est là-bas.'*)

- *Play your cards right*
  Visual aids are concealed one at a time (e.g. flashcards reversed), and the class have to guess the identity of each in turn. This is effective if played as a team game.

- *Blockbusters*
  Pupils guess the vocabulary/structures from initials on a grid. Also relies on memory (see below).

Memory games

Learners are given opportunities to commit items to long-term memory.

- *Kim's game*
  Visual aids are displayed; one is removed; pupils have to identify which one. Powerpoint and the OHP can be used here.

- *I went to the market*
  Pupils take turns to add to the list of new lexical items, which have to be remembered and repeated in order, within a sentence. This works well with shopping vocabulary, and the structure *J'ai acheté/ich habe . . . gekauft*, but should not be restricted to this topic.

  Conveyor belt (as in The Generation Game)
  A series of images is moved across the screen (Powerpoint or on an OHP transparency), and pupils work in teams to remember as many as possible (see Harris *et al.*, 2001)

  Who wants to be a millionaire?
  Computer software is available for this, although it can also be played using cards.

Interaction activities

Opportunities need to be created for pupil:pupil as well as teacher:pupil interaction.

- *Distributing visual aids*
  Pupils ask for items using structures presented. If they then conceal these, others can be charged with the task of recovering them by using the appropriate language.

- *Pupils as teacher*
  When sufficiently confident about new language, pupils may act as the teacher by working on the interactive whiteboard, or manipulating the flashcards, for the benefit of the class.

Activity 3.3

Using the outcomes of Activities 3.1 and 3.2, the aim of this activity is to sequence the activities at the presentation stage of the lessons.

(A) Describe the activities which would be possible with the resources, and why these would maximise their potential effectiveness.

Resource	Activity	Rationale (pupil motivation, etc.)

Activity 3.3 *continued*

Resource	Activity	Rationale (pupil motivation, etc.)

(B)   Organise the list of activities above into an appropriate sequence, with reference to the phases in presenting new language identified in the chapter. Consider teacher and pupil use of target language, including teacher questions and prompts, in each of these phases.

Phase	Activity	Use of target language	
		Teacher	Pupil
Listening			
Repeating			
Matching			
Q & A			

Activity 3.3 *continued*

Guessing			
Memory			
Interaction			

(C) Discuss with your mentor how she recognises when pupils are ready to move on to the next phase of the presentation stage. What are the signs, and how can this monitoring be incorporated into the teaching and learning activities?

SUMMARY

When presenting new vocabulary and structures, activities organised by the teacher should be underpinned by knowledge of what is 'learnable', and at what stages of learning particular activities have the greatest impact. The teacher has a wide range of resources available and, therefore, decisions on which resources are most suited to each topic, as well as to each activity, must be made.

USEFUL WEBSITES

Internet Picture Dictionary
www.pdictionary.com/
Language Guide
www.languageguide.org/
MFL Sunderland
www.sunderlandschools.org/mfl-sunderland/resources.htm
Learning and Teaching Scotland MFL
www.ltscotland.org.uk/mfle/resources/index.asp
The Ashcombe School
www.ashcombe.surrey.sch.uk/Curriculum/modlang/index_teaching.htm
www.ashcombe.surrey.sch.uk/Curriculum/modlang/index_primary.htm

Chapter 4   Developing modern foreign language skills through formative assessment

TREVOR MUTTON

Chapter aims

By the end of the chapter you should:

- understand the purposes of different techniques for assessment used in the MFL classroom;
- be aware of a range of strategies and techniques for carrying out formative assessment;
- be aware of the ways in which feedback can be given to learners;
- have an understanding of the potential benefits and some of the issues involved in using formative assessment in the MFL classroom.

WHY DO WE ASSESS PUPILS?

There are a number of reasons why teachers need to assess pupils and these fall broadly into the following categories (see also *Learning to Teach MLF in the Secondary School*, second edition, Routledge):

- to determine the extent to which the learning objectives for any lesson/series of lessons have been met;
- to evaluate how effective specific teaching strategies may have been in bringing about the desired learning;
- to identify what pupils may need to do next in order to develop their learning further;
- to measure performance in relation to other pupils, or in relation to a specific set of criteria;
- to gain external accreditation;
- to predict how pupils may perform (e.g. in external examinations);
- as a tool for increasing motivation;
- to provide the information needed to report on the progress of individual students to others (e.g. parents and carers);
- to inform decisions as to which teaching groups pupils may be placed in.

FORMATIVE AND SUMMATIVE ASSESSMENT

The above purposes could be seen to fall into one of two categories – they could be said to be either *summative* or *formative* in nature.

Summative assessment is often now referred to as assessment *of* learning and is used when a teacher needs to make a judgement about how well a pupil is performing, often against a set of specific criteria (e.g. National Curriculum levels in MFL for each of the four Attainment Targets). The information obtained from summative assessments are often shared with others and may be used to assign a grade or level to pupils, to relate the achievement to national standards, to provide a record of progress over time, to make comparisons in relation to performance across a range of subjects in the school, etc. For this reason the assessment carried out needs to be both valid (i.e. it actually measures what it intends to measure) and reliable (i.e. it is accurate and consistent).

Formative assessment is now often referred to as 'assessment *for* learning' (or AfL) and is used as a diagnostic tool within the classroom. It has been defined by the Assessment Reform Group (2002) as:

> the process of seeking and interpreting evidence for use by learners and their teachers to decide where the learners are in their learning, where they need to go and how best to get there.

This group has also defined the key principles that characterise formative assessment in the classroom and state that assessment for learning should:

- be part of effective planning of teaching and learning;
- focus on how students learn;
- be recognised as central to classroom practice;
- be regarded as a key to professional skill for teachers;
- be sensitive and constructive because any assessment has an emotional impact;
- take account of the importance of learner motivation;
- promote commitment to learning goals and a shared understanding of the criteria by which they are assessed;
- enable learners to receive constructive guidance about how to improve;
- develop learners' capacity for self-assessment so that they can become reflective and self-managing;
- recognise the full range of achievements of all learners.

Formative assessment is defined by Black and Wiliam (1998) as referring to:

> all those activities undertaken by teachers *and by their students in assessing themselves*, which provide information to be used as feedback to modify the teaching and learning activities in which they are engaged. *Such assessment becomes 'formative assessment' when the evidence is actually used to adapt the teaching work to meet the needs.*

Formative assessment is, therefore, an integral part of teaching and learning and is an ongoing process in the classroom.

INTEGRATING FORMATIVE ASSESSMENT INTO PLANNING

Effective formative assessment does not just take place – it needs careful planning and should be integrated into the whole process of teaching and learning (see also Chapter 2). Lesson planning will demonstrate this in a number of ways but primarily it will take into account the information gained from recent pupil learning opportunities (i.e. as a result of any informal or formal assessment carried out in previous lessons and reflection on this), as well

Activity 4.1

Below you will find a list of some assessment tasks that might be carried out in the MFL classroom. First, and with reference to the list provided in this chapter, identify what you think the main *purpose* of each of the assessments might be (see above) and then decide whether this is an example of *formative* or *summative* assessment.

Do any of these activities raise issues about what is actually being assessed and for what purpose?

For those that you identify as being primarily summative in nature, discuss how these might also, where possible, be further used in relation to a formative dimension.

Assessment activity	Purpose	Formative or summative?
Assessing individuals who are involved in a pair work oral activity in which they are discussing likes and dislikes of foods.		
Assessing a reading task in which pupils have to look at a brochure and then respond to true/false statements related to the facilities in a town.		
Assessing a dialogue/short scene in a café where pupils are working as a group and assigning a National Curriculum level to the performance of individuals.		
Monitoring pupil responses to teacher-led questions about family and pets in a whole-class setting.		
A plenary task that involves pupils feeding back on what they have learnt about asking and giving directions.		
Collecting in the marks following a listening exercise in which pupils had to identify the hobbies of a group of native speakers on tape.		

Activity 4.1 *continued*

Assessment activity	Purpose	Formative or summative?
A vocabulary test, focusing on ten items of clothing.		
Assessing a piece of GCSE coursework in which pupils are writing about their school.		
Feedback on a written piece, completed as homework, about what the pupil did last weekend.		
An end of unit test covering all aspects of the topic 'House and Home'.		
A GCSE listening test that is carried out as a practice activity in class.		
An A-level essay related to the issue of young people in the target country.		

as the assessment opportunities that need to be integrated into subsequent lessons for the cycle to continue. A key aspect of this is the identification of appropriate learning objectives and the planning of specific learning outcomes, but even these will then need to be broken up into smaller steps in learning (what we could call 'micro-objectives') and for each of these smaller steps the teacher will have to make a judgement as to what extent the learning within theses micro objectives has been met. This judgement might be as the result of informal monitoring of pupil responses (e.g. gauging the accuracy of pupil responses during a question-and-answer session as part of the presentation phase of the lesson in which new vocabulary is being introduced) but in other cases be more structured (e.g. assessing the work produced from a reading exercise). In both cases, the information gained will be used to inform the teacher of a number of things. For example:

- the extent to which the learning objectives have or have not been met;
- the action that may need to be taken by the teacher to address any issues arising from this analysis;
- the feedback that may need to be given to individual pupils to inform them about specific aspects of their learning.

Activity 4.2

Focus on a lesson / series of lessons that you are soon to teach and plan in detail the way in which you will assess the learning that you want to take place. Think about how you will assess each of the micro objectives, as well as the overall learning objectives in order to get a clearer picture of what the pupils have actually learnt. It might be helpful first to identify the overall learning objectives, then the smaller steps (the micro objectives) that will lead to the planned learning taking place, then the activities you might use to bring about the learning and, finally, how the learning will be assessed. Below is an example.

Topic: House and Home

Learning objectives: pupils will know the names of the rooms in the house and be able to describe what rooms they have in their own house.

Micro-objective	Activity	Assessment opportunities
Revision of previous work	Game to revise *'à la campagne'*, *'en ville'* etc.	Monitoring pupil contributions
Become familiar with the sounds of the new vocabulary	Introduce new language using PowerPoint presentation	Informal monitoring of receptivity
Practise pronunciation	Repetition and question-and-answer sequence	Informal monitoring of responses

etc.

and later in the lesson:

Use the new language in a structured dialogue	Group work activity, with pupils working in threes to carry out dialogues in pairs using questions and answers to ascertain details of where the other lives	Teacher: monitoring to assess recall of vocabulary and accuracy of pronunciation. Peer assessment: one pupil in the group (in turn) to monitor and assess the responses
Use the new language independently	Written activity – using a writing frame to generate pupils account of their own house / flat, etc.	Assessment of written work and in-depth feedback comments

SELF-ASSESSMENT AND PEER-ASSESSMENT

Self-assessment and peer-assessment should be seen as valuable tools in the classroom and ones that can have an impact on the way that pupils learn as part of the overall framework of formative assessment in the MFL classroom. This can be achieved through increased levels of learner autonomy, through collaborative learning (since pupils are discussing together specific aspects of their work and providing the opportunity to learn from each other through feedback) and through pupils being able to reflect on and share specific learning strategies.

However, the integration of self-assessment and peer-assessment is not a straightforward matter and depends on pupils being equipped with the necessary understanding and skills to carry out such activities effectively. These will include:

- a knowledge of the learning goals towards which they have been working;
- an understanding of the criteria by which the assessments are being carried out;
- a model in their heads of what a good piece of work might look like;
- practice in applying criteria to specific pieces of work;
- the ability to give positive feedback to help another learner develop.

The teacher will clearly need to make the learning goals and the criteria explicit, and model how the self-assessment and peer-assessment process might work. The skills can be taught gradually, through practice, once the initial expectation of working in this way has been established. The following are suggestions as to how peer-assessment activities might be approached in relation to specific MFL activities, but all depend to some extent on the pupils having the knowledge, understanding and skills as described above.

Speaking activities

- Asking the class to assess oral presentations that groups of pupils, or individuals, have produced.
- Asking pupils to devise their own criteria for assessing an oral performance, based on their understanding of the learning goals, and then asking them to apply these.
- Asking pupils to assess each other in groups of three; two pupils will perform a pair work task and the other pupil will carry out an assessment of one or both of the others, perhaps recording the results on a sheet (see Pachler and Field, 2001, p. 220 for an example of what such a sheet might look like).
- As above, but one pupil will give a short presentation to the other two, who will assess the performance and then discuss the results together.

Writing activities

- Before asking pupils to write a particular piece, provide an example with anticipated errors in it that pupils correct individually, or in pairs, providing as they do so reasons for their choices.
- Give group feedback by using a text you have written that contains the most common errors that pupils have made and correct as above.
- Produce a list of words in pairs, with a correct and an incorrect version (based on errors that pupils may have made) and correct as above.
- Allow pupils to discuss a piece of completed work before it is handed in to see if one pupil could discover any errors in another pupil's work and vice versa.

Reading and listening activities

- Pupils review their work together after it is completed and discuss where any improvements could be made.

- Pupils discuss together what they have found difficult/straightforward in the task and provide feedback to you (possibly using 'traffic lighting'); pupils discuss together what strategies they have used in dealing with the text in question.

Activity 4.3

Using the list of activities from Activity 4.1 again, this time identify how each of these assessment opportunities might be developed in order to incorporate peer assessment and / or self-assessment in a meaningful and productive way.

Discuss any of the issues that arise from taking such an approach and how these might be successfully addressed.

Assessment activity	Use of peer assessment / self-assessment
Assessing individuals who are involved in a pair work oral activity in which they are discussing likes and dislikes of foods.	
Assessing a reading task in which pupils have to look at a brochure and then respond to true/false statements related to the facilities in a town.	
Assessing a dialogue / short scene in a café where pupils are working as a group and assigning a National Curriculum level to the performance of individuals.	
Monitoring pupil responses to teacher-led questions about family and pets in a whole-class setting.	
A plenary task that involves pupils feeding back on what they have learnt about asking and giving directions.	
Collecting in the marks following a listening exercise in which pupils had to identify the hobbies of a group of native speakers on tape.	
A vocabulary test, focusing on ten items of clothing.	
Assessing a piece of GCSE coursework in which pupils are writing about their school.	

Activity 4.3 *continued*

Assessment activity	Use of peer assessment / self-assessment
Feedback on a written piece, completed as homework, about what the pupil did last weekend.	
An end-of-unit test covering all aspects of the topic 'House and Home'.	
A GCSE listening test that is carried out as a practice activity in class.	
An A-level essay related to the issue of young people in the target country.	

Now look at the scheme of work or your own medium-term plans for a unit of work that you will soon be teaching and identify specific activities where peer or self-assessment might be incorporated, and the precise ways in which you see this working.

GIVING FEEDBACK TO PUPILS

Teachers spend a significant amount of time assessing pupils' work and marking is often seen as a time-consuming, so it is important that assessment of pupil work is done as effectively as possible. Whilst some assessment will, by its nature, be more summative than formative (e.g. marking end-of-unit assessments), a lot of what the teacher does can be categorised as the latter and be seen as assessment *for* learning (as opposed to assessment *of* learning). This can contribute to the pupils' development of their language skills in two ways: first, the teacher will use the information gained from assessing the work to inform future planning that will take into account what pupils have learnt and what they still need to learn; and second, it will enable the teacher to give *individualised* feedback to pupils. Clearly there is not time to provide in-depth individualised feedback on each piece of work that the pupil produces in each of the four skills. It should, however, be possible to use a range of assessment strategies according to the nature of the task being assessed, the purposes of the assessment, etc. It may be useful to consider two levels of assessment:

1   *Overview assessments*, which might entail the following:

- a check that the activity has been completed;
- a snapshot impression as to whether the learning objectives have been met and to what extent planning needs to be amended in the light of the pupils' performance on the task;

- a brief analysis of how the pupil has performed;
- a brief analysis of any areas that need further development;
- brief, general feedback.

2   *In-depth assessments*, which would be characterised by:

- a more detailed analysis of the strengths of the piece of work;
- an analysis of the key areas for development;
- full written feedback that provides details of the strengths of the piece, one or two specific areas that the pupil might need to work on as a result of the feedback, and suggestions as to how the pupil might achieve this improvement (including suggestions for learning strategies);
- the facilitation of a dialogue between pupil and teacher, with the teacher possibly asking questions to which the pupil subsequently responds (e.g. 'What do you have to remember about the past participle in a German sentence?');
- an absence of error correction, but rather a limited number of errors being high-lighted, all of which relate to the learning point on which the teacher is focusing.[1]

Activity 4.4

Look at the piece of work below from a Year 10 pupil. (The task was to describe a recent holiday.)

How would you go about assessing this piece of work in a way that would place the emphasis on the principles of formative assessment?

What would you highlight as being the strengths of the piece? What specific error(s) would you decide to focus on? Precisely what in-depth feedback would you give?

If you discovered that some of the errors are characteristic of the work of a number of pupils in the class, how might you approach the issues when giving general feedback to the class, or adapt the next stage of your teaching to take into account this information?

Account of a holiday

L'année dernière ma famille et me suis allé à l'Italie sur les vacances pour deux semaines, nous sommes restés dans une villa avec sa proper piscine, la villa était stupéfiante et il avait une belle vue des montagnes, c'était trés chaud et ensoleillé pour le premièrement coupler de jours que nous venons de relâcher et sommes allès nager, sur la deuxième samaine nous avons loué une voiture et avons conduit environ visitant des villes, pendant les vacances nous avons dépensé beaucoup de temps commercial et nageant c'était grand! A l'avenir j'aimerais rentrer à l'Italie parce que c'est stupéfaint, il faisait chaud et j avais un vraiment bon temps.

GIVING FEEDBACK IN RELATION TO THE OTHER LANGUAGE LEARNING SKILLS

Whilst it is relatively easy to incorporate formative feedback into one's assessment practices in relation to writing tasks, it is perhaps less straightforward when it comes to the other language skills.

Speaking

The majority of feedback given in relation to speaking tasks tends to be immediate and given orally. It is, however, worth considering the possibility of giving feedback in *writing* from time to time (from experience, I would say that pupils who have received such feedback tend to value it and to use it as a real focus for developing their learning since they have time to digest it fully and reflect on what needs to be done and go back to it if necessary).

There are clearly issues that have to be addressed when considering how to make full use of oral assessments in order to promote learning in the classroom.

Activity 4.5

What are the issues that might constrain the effective use of assessing oral work in the classroom? In what ways might these be addressed? Add to the list below and suggest solutions that might facilitate such assessment.

Issue	What can be done?
It is impossible to get around all the pupils in one lesson	Spread the assessments over a period of time – aim for one 'in-depth' assessment per pupil for each unit of work
The assessment will not be valid if individual pupils are assessed at different times and at different stages of the unit	It does not matter since the purpose of the assessment is *not to provide summative data* but to *develop the learning of the individual pupil* through the assessment and feedback process
Other pupils may need my help whilst I am trying to assess two pupils involved in a pair work task	
Others?	

Listening and reading

It appears to be fairly common practice in some MFL classrooms to carry out a listening activity that involves the pupils recording their responses in some way (completing a grid; indicating true/false phrases, etc.) and then for the teacher to go through the exercise and get the pupils to 'mark' their work. At the end the results may be collected in or a show of hands indicates the pupils who got 8, 7, 6, etc. items correct. Such assessment data gives little information. If an individual pupil gets a mark of 4 out of a possible 6, for example, this does not tell the teacher which two items the pupil had difficulty with, or whether all the pupils who achieved the same mark had difficulty with the same two items. Although some course books may attach a National Curriculum level to the task, the collection of marks alone fails to give any qualitative information that might inform future teaching and learning.

Rather than assessing all listening (or reading) activities in a similar way it would be preferable to plan which tasks in these skills will be designated as assessment activities from which you gain appropriate information about the learning process. It is not easy to give detailed feedback in relation to these skills but it is nevertheless possible, and the following might be ways of achieving this:

- Monitor a number of individual pupils whilst they are doing listening or reading exercises and note the ways in which they are working.
- Collect in the work that is produced and analyse what they seem to do well/less well.
- Focus on the use of learner strategies – get pupils to tell you how they approach tasks and the strategies they use and relate feedback to their apparent effectiveness.
- Get pupils to comment on their own performance in writing after the task has been completed and respond to these comments.

Activity 4.6

Fill in the table below, identifying the different types of assessment for listening (L) and reading (R) activities that you could use. In each case, identify which skill the activity relates to and then think about what the pupils are being required to do in order for you to assess their level of comprehension. Which are well-suited (or less well-suited) to being used as formative assessment activities?

Assessment activity	L/R?	What are the pupils doing?	Issues in relation to formative assessment
e.g. A text comprising a series of single sentences (each numbered) describing hobbies	L or R	Matching the information in the text to pictures (with a designated letter)	Useful as a practice activity but less effective as a formative assessment activity because it is difficult to identify which aspect of the task may have been easy/less easy for the pupil.
e.g. A text focusing on a number of teenagers in the target country describing hobbies, including other related details (frequency, cost, the people with whom the hobby is carried out, etc.)	L or R	Completing a table summarising the key information in relation to each of the speakers/writers	Opportunity to assess the outcomes and give pupils feedback based on their strengths and the areas they need to develop in terms of their listening / reading skills. Opportunity to discuss strategies for effective listening / reading with individuals or the whole class.

Activity 4.6 *continued*

Assessment activity	L/R?	What are the pupils doing?	Issues in relation to formative assessment
			Opportunity to give group feedback in relation to common errors / misconceptions. Opportunities for peer and/ or self-assessment.
etc.			

SUMMARY

The conscious use of formative assessment (or assessment for learning) in the classroom can be an invaluable tool to help develop the pupils' foreign language skills. It is, however, an approach that needs to be integrated fully into the language learning process and will only be effective if there is an underlying understanding of the principles behind it and a commitment to putting these principles into practice in the classroom. Research has shown that such an approach leads to improvements in levels of attainment (Black and Wiliam, 1998) and it is also not difficult to see the positive effect that it can have on levels of pupil motivation. If we are to raise the levels of achievement of the pupils we teach then we should be keen to develop our own practice in this area and provide pupils with overwhelmingly positive experiences of the assessment process.

NOTE

1 Studies have shown that providing detailed error correction for learners has limited effect in terms of producing correct language in future work and that learners do not produce a greater number of errors when no corrections are given (see Macaro 2003). Although giving in-depth feedback takes time, it might be worth considering the time saved by not providing detailed error correction, and which of these options is most likely to lead to gains in pupil learning.

USEFUL WEBSITES

Assessment in general

www.gtce.org.uk/shared/rotm/103260/standstudy.pdf

This is a General Teaching Council for England (GTCE) 'Research of the Month' site focusing on Black and Wiliam's study (1998) *'Inside the Black Box'*.

www.gtce.org.uk/shared/rotm/103260/rom_19_AFL.pdf

A second GTCE 'Research of the Month' site, focusing on Black *et al.* (2003), following up the work of the above study.

www.qca.org.uk/7659.html

The Qualification and Curriculum Authority (QCA) site is useful in providing a summary of the work of the Assessment Reform Group and an outline of the principles of Assessment for Learning.

www.arg.educ.cam.ac.uk

The Assessment Reform Group website that gives extensive details of the development of recent assessment practices in the United Kingdom and also includes information about current national research projects.

www.ltscotland.org.uk/assess/

The website of Assessment is for Learning (AiFL), which provides information about the development of formative assessment techniques in Scotland, including links to case studies, research, etc.

www.ofsted.gov.uk/publications/index.cfm?fuseaction=pubs.displayfile&id=3205&type=pdf

A link to the Ofsted report entitled *Good Assessment in Secondary Schools*.

www.standards.dfes.gov.uk/keystage3

The National Strategy website has lots of information on formative assessment. A search under 'Assessment for Learning' will provide a range of different resources.

Assessment specifically related to MFL

www.ofsted.gov.uk/publications/index.cfm?fuseaction=pubs.displayfile&id=3214&type=doc

A link to the Ofsted report entitled *Good Assessment Practice in Modern Foreign Languages*.

www.teachers.tv/subjectBlockVideo.do?transmissionBlockId=210618&zoneId=2&transmissionProgrammeId=211925

A link to two programmes from teachers' TV that focus on the use of assessment in the MFL classroom.

www.ltscotland.org.uk/mfle/currentinitiatives/assessmentisforlearning/index.asp

Another link to the Scottish AiFL website, in this case with specific reference to formative assessment in MFL.

Part 2　Developing key skills, knowledge and understanding

Chapter 5 Developing listening skills in the modern foreign language

GARY CHAMBERS

Chapter aims

By the end of this chapter you should:

- have a clear understanding of the complexity of listening;
- have gained some insight into the factors which may make listening difficult for some pupils;
- have an understanding of how to exploit a listening text as a 'learning experience' rather than a 'test';
- have acquired some ideas for listening tasks which might put the pupils more in control of their own listening.

WHAT IS IT AND WHY BOTHER WITH IT?

What is it?

As a student, I spent my summers working as a labourer on a building site. Each year one of my naïve fellow students was invariably sent by one of the tradesmen to the supplies hut for 'a long stand'. The worker in charge of supplies, familiar with the joke, told the unsuspecting student to wait. Of course the student was made to wait and wait and wait – a long stand.

What lessons can be learned from this?

- Speaker and listener have to be operating within the same context for understanding to be facilitated. Could the student have known that the tradesman was playing a joke? Did the student know what a 'long stand' was, what it looked like or why it was needed?
- The listener should take advantage of any visual clues which may be on offer. Was the tradesman smirking as he gave the instruction? Was there a glint in his eye? Was there anything about his body language which suggested that something was not quite right?
- What about aural clues, such as tone of voice?

Listening is neither a simple nor a passive activity. It is not just a matter of 'switching on' the ears and letting it happen. The listener has to bring much to the listening:

- knowledge of the topic of the listening text;
- knowledge of the language;
- the ability to recognise and discriminate between individual sounds;
- the ability to pick out the main points from the redundant material;
- the ability to fill in gaps left by the speaker.

Listening is very much a complex and an active activity.

Why bother with it?

Listening is integral to the language learning process. Listening rarely takes place in isolation from other skills and usually happens in tandem with them, most commonly speaking. It is a rich source of material for consolidating known language and giving access to unknown language which can (and often should) be recycled. It has a contribution to make to pupils' listening skills in general, not just the foreign language. This is reflected in the skills identified in the Key Stage 3 National Strategy; for example, listening for gist and detail (7L3), listening for subtleties (8L1), listening for inferences (9L1), recognising rhetorical devices (9L2). Listening material can be found in an interesting and varied range of sources (TV, film, video, radio, theatre, internet, conversation), contributing to learning in general, interests and hobbies, cultural insights and entertainment.

WHAT MAKES IT DIFFICULT?

In survey after survey, pupils put listening activities at the bottom or next to the bottom (after writing) of their list of most enjoyed MFL activities (see Chambers, 1993, 1998). Ask a group of Year 9 pupils what they think of listening tasks and this may be how they reply:

'The tapes are always crap. I can't hear the voices properly.'
'The cassette recorder never works properly.'
'Germans speak too fast'
'The exercises are too hard for me'

The equipment may well be inadequate. This issue can be addressed relatively easily with appropriate investment. It may also be the case that the equipment is fine but that the pupils are being inadequately prepared for the task in hand. This is more than likely the reason why pupils perceive the Germans (and other nationalities) as speaking too fast or the exercises as being too difficult.

In a large furniture store I passed by a customer who asked her partner: 'Have you seen those delicious suites?' Imagine that this had been recorded for use in a language learning class. Given that the recording would probably be on audio tape, the pupils would not have access to the clues they would need to make them aware of the context. They would also need to have quite sophisticated knowledge of language to distinguish between 'suites' and 'sweets' and to recognise the interesting use of 'delicious'. The chances are that the teacher, rather than the pupils, would have control of the replay facility and would determine how much was heard at one go and how often the whole tape was heard. Is it any wonder pupils find listening difficult?

Listening is challenging. Your chances to hear the text are limited (probably by someone else). You need to bring so much scaffolding to the experience:

- knowledge of the context;
- knowledge of the topic;
- knowledge of language.

If pupils are to enjoy listening activities, their knowledge of the above areas needs to be triggered as part of the preparation for the activity. To fail to do so, leads to pupils tackling the activity 'cold', without the knowledge that they would normally have in an authentic listening context. When they go to the bakery in their home town, for example, they are aware of the sort of language they are going to hear and use. When they go to the bakery in a French town, they will probably rehearse the language they are going to use on the way to the bakery and predict the sort of language they are going to hear; visual clues (facial expression; body language; pointing) will also be available to support understanding and communication.

How can we move more towards providing pupils with the scaffolding they need to succeed in and enjoy listening activities?

LISTENING AS A TEST *VERSUS* LISTENING AS A LEARNING EXPERIENCE

You hand out the worksheet; you tell the pupils to be quiet, to listen to the tape (to be played twice) and to tick the boxes as appropriate; you go through the answers with the pupils. This is a very crude version of a listening test. It could be made less crude. Instructions could be given in the target language. You might go through the worksheet to ensure understanding. The task might be something more imaginative than ticking boxes. Nevertheless, it is a test. Tests do have their place. After all, pupils will have to engage in listening tests at GCSE, AS and A2 levels. If, however, we want listening to rise up the league table of favoured activities and pupils to become more skilled listeners, tests should not be the norm. Tests should be transformed into learning experiences (see White, 2001: 10).

Before looking at an example of a learning experience based on a listening text, there are a number of principles, some of which might usefully be shared with pupils, to enhance their understanding of the listening process and of the strategies which might be employed:

- Pupils are more likely to be receptive to listening texts and tasks, if their purpose is made clear. White (2001: 5) describes a study of native speakers by Bone (1988): people often listen at only 25 per cent of their potential and ignore, forget, distort or mis-understand the other 75 per cent. Concentration rises above 25 per cent if they think that what they are hearing is important and/or they are interested in it, but it never reaches 100 per cent.
- They do not have to understand every word in order to understand the essence of the text. Depending on our perception of what we need to understand (consider the difference between listening to instructions on how to drive a car and listening to the evening news), we listen as extensively as possible and intensively as necessary.
- Listening is not a passive but an active process.
- Strategies for understanding include: concentrating on what is understood; distin-guishing between the important and the unimportant; exploitation of what is already known about the topic.
- A relaxed atmosphere opens up all the senses (see Solmecke, 1992: 10).
- The level of difficulty is determined not by the text but by the task.
- Hypothesis testing is part of learning to listen (and of learning a language). It is OK to get something wrong. We learn from our mistakes.

LISTENING AS A LEARNING EXPERIENCE – A CONCRETE EXAMPLE

Meine Woche

Am Montag fahre ich Fahrrad.	*On Monday I ride my bike.*
Am Dienstag sehe ich fern.	*On Tuesday I watch TV.*
Am Mittwoch spiele ich Fußball.	*On Wednesday I play football.*
Das mache ich sehr, sehr gern.	*I like that very much.*
Am Donnerstag, da schwimmen wir.	*On Thursday we go swimming.*
Am Freitag spiele ich Klavier.	*On Friday I play piano.*

Am Samstag kommt Frau Stange.	*On Saturday Frau Stange comes.*
Am Sonntag schlafe ich lange.	*On Sunday I have a lie in.*
Und schon höre ich die Mama:	*And already I can hear my mum:*
'Komm Peter! Steh auf! Schule!'	*'Come on Peter. Get up. Time for school!'*
Ja, dann ist der Montag da.	*Yes, it's Monday.*

(Source: Seeger, H. (1985))

Pre-listening phase

As the term suggests, the pre-listening phase precedes the first playing of the recording. The purpose of pre-listening activities is to:

- put the text into context;
- stimulate pupils' knowledge of the topic;
- stimulate the pupils' knowledge of language associated with the topic;
- arouse expectations of what the text might contain;
- arouse curiosity.

Such activities might include:

- discussion of a picture:
- a short piece of reading:
- brain-storming:
- setting a scene and asking the pupils to predict what happens next.

(For many more examples see Underwood, 1989: 44; Dahlhaus, 1994.)

Activity 5.1

Looking at the poem above, think of possible pre-listening activities.
Consider the following questions:

- How are you going to access how much vocabulary the pupils already know about free-time activities?
- How are you going to make them curious about the poem they are going to read a little later in the lesson?
- How are you going to introduce key words contained in the poem, which will help the pupils understand the poem?

Suggestions:

- Put a diary in a bag; invite a pupil to come to the front of the class; show her/ him the contents; the rest of the class then has to establish what is in the bag by asking questions which may only be answered by 'yes' or 'no'. Depending on the level of ability of the class, this might be done in the target language. This could then lead to revision of days, months, possible diary entries.
- Thought-shower/brainstorming/*Wortigel* (spidergram) – on the topic of spare-time activities.
- Provide the pupils with six or seven key words which come up in the poem (e.g. *Montag/Mittwoch/Samstag/Frau Stange/Klavier/Fußball/Schule*) and ask them to write a short story that includes these words.

For other pre-listening ideas, see Dahlhaus (1994).

While-listening phase

In this phase the text is played to the pupils for the first time. It has two parts. Part 1 includes activities to access pupils' global understanding of the text, its broad content and/or general message. It also gives pupils the opportunity to tune into the speed at which people speak, their mood, accent and any background noises. Activities, therefore, usually take the form of broad questions, such as:

- How many people are speaking?
- Where are they?
- Are they happy/sad/angry?

See also Dahlhaus (1994) and www.zut.org.uk. This website provides a host of activities (French-related) which could easily be adapted to provide tasks which access pupils' global understanding.

Again, depending on the pupils' level of language, this phase may be conducted in the target language. They should be made aware that they will hear the tape as often as they need to.

The answers provided by the pupils can of course be developed further (in the target language) to revise more known material; for example, what's the second/fifth/sixth day of the week? Can we think of six other German names? Can we remember five other activities without looking at the spidergram?

Activity 5.2

Thinking about the poem on pages 52–3, what might you use as appropriate while-listening activities to access *global understanding*?
Consider the following questions:

- What activities would give the pupils a reason to listen to the text without forcing them to listen to detailed information or language with which they might not be familiar?
- Could a kinaesthetic approach be adopted?

Suggestions

- Put your hand up when you hear a day of the week.
- Stand up when you hear someone's name.
- How many of the activities on the spidergram do you hear on the tape?

Now that the pupils are tuned into the pace, context and language of the tape, they are ready for while-listening Part 2, which accesses their detailed understanding of the text.
Such activities might include:

- questions and answers in English/German;
- true/false;
- multiple choice;
- listen and draw;
- listen and follow the instructions;
- listen and identify the face/person/animal which matches the description;
- listen and fill in the gap in the text.

Again, pupils should be made aware that they will hear the tape as often as they need to.

Activity 5.3

Looking at the poem, what sort of activities might be appropriate in this phase for accessing *detailed understanding*?
Consider the following:

- What language do you want the pupils to remember and recycle (see post-listening phase)?
- What activities would allow you to stay in the target language but still access pupils' comprehension of the text (rather than facilitate regurgitation of sections of the text)?
- Can you think of an activity which might be just a little bit different?

Suggestions:

- Listen and put the jumbled text/jumbled pictures in the appropriate order.
- Correct the factual inaccuracies.
- Fill in the missing activities in the appropriate gaps in the transcript/chart.
- Answer the questions in German.
- Mime the activities as you hear them.

You may wish to try out other while-listening activities at the following websites:

www.zut.org.uk
www.bbc.co.uk/schools/gcsebitesize

Post-listening phase

In the course of the pre- and while-listening activities, pupils will have consolidated known vocabulary and perhaps grammatical structures (e.g. verb inversion) and accessed some new language. The post-listening phase should be exploited to recycle this. How might this be done in the case of the poem, *Meine Woche*?

Activity 5.4

Consider the following:

- How can the listening text stimulate a multi-skill learning experience, that is, one which includes one or more of listening, speaking, writing and reading?
- Is there an opportunity here for pair and group work?
- Can we provide pupils, in this phase, with a real or plausible reason to speak/write/read?

Suggestions

- Pupils write their own poem, based on the structure of *Meine Woche*.
- With their partner, they write a dialogue based on what they do each day.

Activity 5.4 *continued*

- They write a letter to their class-link in Germany or to another set in their year group (a 'real' readership) about what they do in their spare time.

Putting the pupils in control

Nothing is so good that it cannot be improved. White (2001: 5) identifies some problems with the above procedure:

- Classroom listening very often put the students in the position of 'passive overhearers' – artificiality of listening to tape; the listener cannot stop, interrogate or interact; the teacher is in control.
- Not much time spent actually listening to the tape – quite a lot on discussing the answers and doing transfer activities.
- Not much time is spent analysing what went wrong – how do students mishear or fail to hear? – we focus on the product of listening rather than the process.

White (2001: 5) suggests that approaches should be adopted which allow pupils to:

- reflect on their problems in understanding and on strategies they could use to overcome problems. This can only be taught effectively by interrupting the listening process and getting students to reflect on what they have just been doing;
- become active participants in the listening process rather than 'passive overhearers';
- control the equipment;
- give the instructions;
- choose what they listen to;
- design the listening tasks;
- make their own listening materials.

Activity 5.5

How can some of the above be addressed in practical terms?
   Suggestions:

- Pupils record an interview with their exchange class to be published in the departmental German/French/Spanish magazine.
- Pupils make a radio play in groups – others have to judge which is best.
- Listening task as part of carousel of activities.
- Exploitation of software and/or internet as source of listening texts.
- Listening homework – pupils use walkman/DVD/video/CD-ROM.
- Pupils provide exercises to go with texts.
- Provide a box of differentiated listening materials, following the model of *Bibliobus* and *Lesekiste* for pupils to access themselves in the course of an autonomous listening session. Pupils could contribute to this, for example, by providing listening materials they may have come across themselves; developing exploitation tasks to accompany the texts; writing critiques of the texts/tasks. Morgan and Neil (2001: 82) provide some useful ideas involving the foreign language assistant (FLA) who could record and provide the following:

Activity 5.5 *continued*

- ✔ 'talking books'
- ✔ tongue-twisters and nursery rhymes
- ✔ listening discrimination exercises
- ✔ 'attitude' tapes where things are said demonstrating different emotions
- ✔ pop songs and accompanying transcriptions

SUMMARY

Listening plays an integral role in the language learning process. Pupils currently do not see Attainment Target 1 as motivating or enjoyable. Even the 'success stories', those who continue with language beyond GCSE, find listening difficult and anxiety-inducing (Graham, 1997). Something has to be done to change this state of affairs. I maintain that a 'learning experience' approach, even with its faults, is more likely to reach the parts of pupils' motivation, that the 'test' cannot reach. Combine this with putting the pupils more in control, and their perceptions of listening could change for the better.

USEFUL WEBSITES

A good starting point for giving pupils more control of their listening might be: www. ashcombe.surrey.sch.uk/Curriculum/modlang/index_teaching.htm. This site provides more than 80 mini videos in French, German, Spanish and Italian with interactive self-marking quizzes. Students have the facility to start, stop and pause the videos as they feel the need and can also access hints for support.

www.languageguide.org contains a range of listening material (with transcripts) on a variety of topics in a number of languages. This site allows pupils to work on tasks related to their own textbook.
www.bonjourdefrance.com/n7/a11/htm provides differentiated materials and accompanying tasks and gives pupils access to definitions of vocabulary in the target language and explanation of grammar points.

The following site includes many very interesting links including those to radio and slide shows with accompanying audio commentary: www.modernlanguages.pwpblueyonder. co.uk/musselburgh/french/sgrade.htm

For foreign language radio and video material with audio commentary try www.bbc.co.uk/languages
www.euronews.net provides authentic video/audio clips with summaries and transcripts.

Chapter 6

Developing speaking skills in the modern foreign language

SUZANNE GRAHAM

Chapter aims

By the end of this chapter you should have:

- gained insights into common problems associated with speaking in the foreign language;
- acquired some ideas for overcoming these problems;
- a clear understanding of what makes a successful speaking activity;
- learnt how to incorporate such activities into the framework of a lesson.

THE CHALLENGE OF ORAL WORK

Research into pupils' perceptions of speaking in the foreign language presents us with something of a paradox. Anecdotal evidence suggests that most learners feel that being able to communicate orally is an important goal in foreign language learning. It is something that many learners see as enjoyable (Chambers, 1999). Yet it is also the skill in which learners at the end of Key Stage 4 feel they have had the least success (Graham, 2002). OFSTED (2004) reports that many pupils lack confidence in speaking at length or with fluency, with few showing the ability to use the target language independently.

Activity 6.1

What is expected of learners nationally in terms of speaking skills? Consult the National Curriculum for England or Wales and a GCSE specification. Outline the types of speaking skills pupils are expected to develop and how progression in speaking is characterised.

Activity 6.1 *continued*

National Curriculum Programme of Study	Progression in speaking in the National Curriculum	Progression in speaking at GCSE
e.g. Programme of Study 2c (DfEE/QCA (1999): 'Pupils should be taught how to ask and answer questions'; 2d: . . . 'how to initiate and develop conversations'	Progression in speaking is characterised by (e.g.) 'improved pronunciation' See www.ncaction.org.uk/ subjects/mfl/progress.htm	Progression in speaking is characterised by (e.g.) 'increased ability to deal with unpredictable elements' See Edexcel (2003: 24–9), grade and assessment criteria for speaking.

Activity 6.2

Think back to classes you have observed in Years 9, 10 or 11. Do you agree with the judgement of OFSTED (2004) that pupils lack confidence in speaking at length with fluency, or independently? If so, what factors might contribute to pupils' under-developed speaking skills?

_____

_____

Reasons you might suggest for pupils' under-developed speaking skills are:

- learners are given speaking tasks that fail to motivate them to speak;
- during speaking tasks, learners engage in off-task behaviour, and revert to the mother tongue;

- lessons that offer learners few opportunities to use the language independently or spontaneously;
- anxiety on the part of learners, which makes them reluctant to take risks in using the language, perhaps for fear of making a mistake or losing face in front of peers;
- speaking tasks are set which are beyond learners' language capabilities;
- teacher-fronted lessons which offer limited opportunities for learners to practise their oral skills;
- learners' uncertainty about pronunciation;
- learners' lack of strategies to make up for gaps in their knowledge, to keep the conversation going. (See also Ur, 1996.)

Possible solutions

Looking at the above list, one factor seems to stand out as an area that we need to focus on if we are to be successful in developing learners' speaking skills – the nature of the speaking tasks that we set them. Perhaps more than any other skill (with the exception possibly of writing), for pupils to speak in the foreign language, they have to *want* to speak or be motivated to do so. This seems an obvious statement, but one that unfortunately is not always put into practice.

Activity 6.3

Think back to a speaking activity you have observed or in which you have participated yourself, where learners seemed motivated to speak. Can you identify any factors that might have contributed to making the speaking activity motivating?

_____

_____

EFFECTIVE SPEAKING TASKS

Ur (1996) gives a comprehensive list of factors that are common to successful speaking activities, including: learners talk a lot; participation is evenly distributed; motivation is high; meaningful information is being communicated. It could be argued that the first two of these factors are in turn influenced by the extent to which learners feel comfortable about speaking and uninhibited by any feelings of anxiety. High motivation, too, is dependent on a number of factors, some of which are discussed below.

Anxiety is low and participation is high

Activity 6.4

Arrange to observe a class and focus on the following areas:

- In whole-class speaking activities (for example, question and answer), roughly what proportion of the class gets to speak? Do some pupils never or rarely speak in such situations? Why not, do you think?

Activity 6.4 *continued*

- What kind of language are pupils producing in whole-class situations? Single words, sentences?
- Where pupils produce more extended answers, what kinds of questions have prompted these responses?
- How are errors in whole-class oral work dealt with by the teacher? Are any of the following used?

    ✔ Recast, where the teacher repeats what the pupil has said but corrects the error (with or without emphasis on the corrected part).
    ✔ The teacher tells the learner that an error has been made and asks him/her for a corrected version.
    ✔ The teacher tells the learner that an error has been made and asks the rest of the class for a corrected version.
    ✔ Errors made by individuals are not dealt with at the time but at a later point the teacher draws the attention of the whole class to errors which are common to many in the group.

- Which of these techniques seem to be the most effective in terms of a) protecting learners' confidence in speaking, b) actually helping learners to avoid the error another time?
- When learners are engaged in pair or group speaking activities, do they make more or fewer errors than in whole-class speaking situations?
- Does the teacher do anything to correct any errors made in pair or group activities?

From your observations you have probably concluded that most learners feel less comfortable when speaking in a whole-class situation than when discussing in a pair or small group. Even adults find the second situation the least anxiety-inducing and the most conducive to the free expression of opinions. This is equally true, if not more so, for those whom Chambers (1999: 127) calls 'image-conscious teenagers', who need to be 'spared the potential perceived humiliation of speaking in a strange tongue before an audience of 25+ peers'.

As well as lowering pupil anxiety, speaking activities that involve pair or small group work have another big advantage over whole-class work – they increase the amount of time that each learner spends speaking the target language. Choral repetition does allow lots of learners to speak at once, but rarely involves learners using the language in anything but an imitative and rather narrow way. In question-and-answer work, open-ended questions give pupils some opportunities to speak at greater length.

Another benefit of pair/group speaking activities is the impact that interaction and negotiation of meaning can have on language acquisition (Lightbown, 2003). Beginning teachers often worry that by working with peers, learners will somehow 'catch' each others' errors. As Lightbown points out, there is very little research evidence to support this view. Indeed, if learners are to be encouraged to take risks with their speaking, the teacher needs to promote a classroom environment in which errors are regarded as part of the learning process and are corrected with sensitivity.

Purpose

Unfortunately, not all learners will value a speaking activity for its own sake, for the good that it might do their oral skills. Most will need an additional reason for completing a task, over and above the fact that you, the teacher, have asked them to complete it and told them that it would be useful for them to do so. In other words, the task needs to have a purpose. It also needs to have an end-goal, so that learners are encouraged to carry it through and not drift into off-task behaviour. In terms of 'purpose', one of the most important attributes of a motivating speaking task is the incorporation of an 'information-gap element'. This means that real information is being exchanged by learners, they are communicating in order to find out something that they need to know. Therefore, in the following activity, learners have to ask questions and give responses in order to determine on which day and at which time they are both free to meet to go out. A separate sheet gives details of possible activities (e.g. films at the cinema, with showing times). At the end of the activity, each pair reports back on when they are meeting and what they are going to do when they meet.

Partenaire A	**Partenaire B**
LUNDI Jean ici 20.00	LUNDI 'Superman' télé 20.15
MARDI Maison des Jeunes 19.00	MARDI
MERCREDI	MERCREDI Cinéma avec Alain 20.45
JEUDI M. Bizet dîner chez nous	JEUDI football télé 19.30
VENDREDI	VENDREDI
SAMEDI barbecue chez Paul 19.00	SAMEDI
DIMANCHE	DIMANCHE chez grands-parents

Reporting back is important for increasing the purpose of activities. Not only do speaking activities need to have a clear end-goal, but learners should also be aware at the start of the activity that the teacher will require some kind of feedback from them (preferably at the end of a predetermined time-limit). This helps to ensure that they actually finish the task and gives it a sense of completeness. Speaking activities that end abruptly, with no follow-up from the teacher or the rest of the class, fail to give such activities the importance that they deserve. Follow-up can take many forms; for example, some pupils might be asked to perform certain aspects of the task to the rest of the class. However, given what was said earlier about how anxiety can inhibit speaking, this should be handled carefully, with clear ground rules established about not laughing at or making fun of the 'performers'. Similarly, for other 'non-performing' learners to listen attentively, the feedback session needs to have a clearly stated purpose. This may be an evaluative one, with the teacher assessing how well learners have dealt with the speaking task. In addition, the class as a whole needs to be aware of the criteria by which the teacher is judging them – are they looking for fluency, accuracy? Furthermore, feedback of this kind is made more effective and perhaps less threatening if it is given not only by the teacher but also by other learners, who might be asked to make suggestions about how the 'performers' could improve what they said, perhaps by paying attention to intonation in question forms (for French), thinking about correct word order (for German).

Clarity and appropriate level of difficulty

One reason that learners stray off-task in speaking activities, perhaps falling back into the mother tongue, is a speaking activity that does not clearly set out what they are expected to do, is not clearly explained by the teacher and requires language beyond their current capability. Take, for example, the following activity, from a published German pairwork resource. Partners A and B both have pictures of four people, but only some of these appear on both partners' sheet. Although the task has a strong information gap element and humour that on the surface makes it a good task, it is not clear what exactly learners have to say, other than that one learner in the pair has to give a description of people met at a party. How the other learner is to react and with what language would need to be explained by the teacher, who would also probably have to pre-teach a number of new phrases to allow learners to respond appropriately.

You (Partner A) went to a party at the weekend at your friend Anna's house. You particularly liked the four people pictured below. Your partner (B) went to a party at Anna's house a while ago and also met four interesting people whose names s/he cannot remember. Are they the same four people? Name and describe each person in turn to see if your partner recognises them. Decide between you whether you met the same four people or not and note down what you decide.

(from Abgemacht!)

Activity 6.5

Look again at the pair-work task outlined above and appropriacy of level of difficulty. Imagine that you wish to use it with a Key Stage 4 class in a unit of work on personal descriptions. Think about the following:

- What question forms would Partner B need to use to check that both partners met the same people?
- What language would Partner B need to confirm whether both partners have met the same people?
- What language would be needed for pupils to report back to the teacher what they have found out?

Opportunities to develop ownership of language

The previous section has emphasised the importance of allowing learners to practise, initially, a fairly limited range of language in a structured situation. However, if learners are to develop the independence that OFSTED (2004) found to be lacking in many classrooms, then activities also need to be provided that take learners beyond this. Learners need to take 'ownership' of the language they are being asked to produce, to personalise it, so that it becomes part of them. This involves more than just talking about themselves in the foreign language – which on its own is not always motivating for learners, particularly if they are conveying such information to a friend who already knows a lot about them! It also requires a restructuring and a manipulation of language that has initially been presented in a guided fashion. Phipps (1999) gives a number of examples of speaking activities that incorporate a creative, 'personalising' element – including asking pupils to substitute their own words for items underlined in a dialogue, ranking items on a list (for example, items one might take to a desert island) and giving reasons for this ranking, adding a problem element to a role play (for example, in a restaurant role play, imagining that you are ordering for a friend who is a vegetarian). Giving a novel twist to transactional topics can also make activities more memorable for learners and allow them to put something of themselves into them. Steven Fawkes (at: http://tre.ngfl.gov.uk) provides a good example of this in the activity summarised below.

Do it in style!

This is a pairwork speaking activity, which requires each actor to take a character card (at random) and perform their script within the character definition given.

Script stimulus

At the railway station

You:	Say good morning
Ticket person:	*responds*
You:	Ask when there is a train for X.
Ticket person:	*responds*
You:	Say you didn't understand
Ticket person:	*responds*
You:	Ask for a single ticket
Ticket person:	*responds*
You:	Say you didn't understand again
Ticket person:	*responds*
You:	Ask how much it costs
Ticket person:	*responds*
You:	Hand over the money

Character cards

1   You are in a *very* good mood.
2   You are very tired.
3   You have drunk too much coffee and are hyperactive.

Developments

- Pupils devise their own character cards.
- Pupils create their own scripts with particular characters in mind.

Characteristics of a good speaking activity: a summary

- The activity is motivating: it has a clear purpose, and an end-goal or outcome.
- Its completion requires language which is within learners' capability.
- Speaking opportunities are maximised, that is, the task cannot be completed by learners saying very little.
- Learners have little scope to revert to the mother tongue.
- The activity can be extended to allow pupils to speak more independently and to personalise the language used.

Activity 6.6

Look at a modern foreign language coursebook and focus on some of the speaking activities it includes. To what extent do they match the criteria for a good speaking activity given in this chapter? If they have any shortcomings, how might you improve them?

_____

_____

INCORPORATING PAIR/GROUP SPEAKING TASKS INTO LESSONS

It is important that before learners are set off on a pair or group speaking task, they have been introduced to and been given supported practice in each element of the language that they will need to complete the activity. So, for example, if they are to conduct a survey to find out what pets classmates have at home, they need to be comfortable in both asking the relevant questions (_Hast du Haustiere? As-tu un animal à la maison?_) and giving a response to such questions.

Phipps (1999) gives detailed guidance in the stages that learners and teachers should go through in moving from whole-class oral work to pair work. The first is likely to involve some kind of modelling by the teacher of each piece of language, probably followed by whole-class repetition. Once the class as a group are comfortable with the language, the exchanges expected in the role play are then practised with the class, with different members of the group having the opportunity to take on each role. For example, in an information-gap activity requiring each partner to find the missing information about a school timetable, the language needed to complete the task in German would be:

Q: _Was hast du am Montag in der ersten Stunde?_
A: _Ich habe Mathe._

The teacher might begin by asking the question to individual pupils (teacher–pupil); then, individual pupils would be asked to pose the question to the teacher (pupil–teacher); next, some 'open pairs' practice might follow, in which a pupil in one part of the classroom would ask the question to another pupil on the other side of the room; finally, the teacher would ask two pupils to demonstrate the role play to the rest of the class, before setting all pupils off on the complete pair work activity with their partner. In this way, pupils are in no doubt about what is required of them in the activity and are confident in the language that they need to use to complete it. However, again, we need to remember that once the language has been practised within such a structured framework, learners should then be given the opportunity to go beyond this.

HELPING LEARNERS TO 'KEEP GOING'

One reason that learners go off-task in speaking activities is that they are unable to sustain their target language use, particularly when they are working on more open-ended speaking tasks that require them to adapt language or deal with the unpredictable – in other words, to use the language more independently. It is thus important to help them to develop communication strategies that enable them to make up for any gaps in their knowledge or skills.

Barnes and Graham (1997: 19–20) outline various ways in which teachers can help learners to develop communication strategies, including teaching them to use filler phrases in the target language (e.g. *alors* in French, *also* in German) to buy time while they endeavour to remember a word that they need in the conversation; the skill of paraphrase or circumlocution, where learners say what they want to say but in different words (for example, if the learner cannot recall the exact phrase in the target language for 'My brother is a vegetarian', he or she might say 'My brother doesn't eat meat'); asking the person they are speaking to repeat or speak more slowly. Barnes and Graham (1997: 20) claim that at GCSE level, many pupils are unable to ask the adult conducting a speaking test with them to repeat or rephrase something they have not understood.

The value of these communication strategies is that they allow learners to stay in the conversation and thus increase their exposure to the target language, and the amount of time they spend using it.

CONCLUSION

Speaking is a language skill which some pupils believe either you are good at or you are not, a skill that in some way is down to personality factors such as confidence or extroversion. In this chapter, I have tried to show that, on the contrary, teachers can enable all learners to acquire the necessary skills to develop their speaking, by carefully selecting and structuring the types of speaking opportunities that they offer to learners, and by helping them to develop strategies that keep them in control when speaking.

USEFUL WEBSITES

Interactive Activities for French Teachers and Learners
www.zut.org.uk

The Ashcombe School
www.ashcombe.surrey.sch.uk/Curriculum/modlang/index_teaching.htm

The Language Guide
www.languageguide.org

Bonjour de France
www.bonjourdefrance.com

FL resources from the BBC
www.bbc.co.uk/languages

FL resources from the Guardian
www.education.guardian.co.uk/netclass/schools/modernlanguages

Really useful French teaching site
www.btinternet.com/~s.glover/S.Glover/languagesite/Default.htm

German for travellers
www.germanfortravellers.com/learn/index2.html

Chapter 7   Use of Storylines to develop reading and writing skills in the modern foreign language

VERNA BRANDFORD

Chapter aims

By the end of this chapter you should:

- have an understanding of the Storyline approach to MFL teaching and learning and its potential;
- be clear about the difference between Storyline and storytelling;
- have acquired ideas for Storylines to develop reading and writing skills.

STORYLINE, WHAT IS IT?

The concept of Storyline was developed in Glasgow, Scotland in response to the Scottish Primary Education Report (1966), which recommended a more holistic teaching approach in history, geography, maths and science. Since then, Storyline has been taught in subjects where the mother-tongue is used as the medium for instruction and interaction.

Although this approach was originally designed to support the teaching of environmental education, it became apparent that 'it also contained principles that supported and encouraged skills practice in many areas of the curriculum. One of these is, importantly, the opportunity for language development and practice' (Bell, 1998).

In Germany, Fehse and Kocher (2002: 199) became aware of the potential of such an approach to motivate learners and to enhance the teaching and learning process in modern foreign languages: 'It allows both teachers and learners to participate in a learning process which is much more open, more creative and less predictable than traditional textbook-based foreign language teaching, but also more structured and therefore more reliable for teachers than the autonomous foreign language classroom.'

The European Comenius-funded project 'Creative Dialogues' (www.creativedialogues. lernnetz.de/) has focused on how, with modifications, the approach might:

- support teaching and learning in the foreign language classroom;
- motivate learners and encourage them to make connections in their learning across the curriculum;
- make a significant contribution to facilitating the transition from primary to secondary language classes that are often perceived as problematic.

Storyline provides an opportunity for pupils to take ownership of their learning. A context is created to help learners feel secure. It provides an audience and a purpose for learning which gives meaning to skills practice that is so often turgid and de-motivating (see Bell, 1998). Motivation, so crucial in the subject, is engendered through involvement of and engagement by learners within a story; for example, 'Best School'. Coyle (2002) comments on the fact that cross-curricular linking in foreign languages is nothing new. It was explicitly promoted in an early draft of the 1990 National Curriculum: 'the full potential of the National Curriculum will only be realized if curricular planning involves the overlap of skills and content across the different subjects' (DES/WO, 1990).

Whilst the teacher has the outline of the Storyline, it is the pupils who will create the detail and content. Implicit in the approach is the notion of the teacher's responsibility to plan the Storyline at the very earliest stages. The aim is to use curricular material (syllabus, scheme of work, National Curriculum requirements, etc.) creatively, imaginatively and purposefully to ensure the cognitive engagement of the pupils. This is achieved through a range of learning opportunities based on specific objectives and learning outcomes which incorporate different abilities and learning styles. The MFL teacher's knowledge of the other curriculum areas and his/her willingness to incorporate relevant aspects into planning and teaching is of paramount importance if pupils are to be encouraged to make connections in their learning; for example, ICT, Design and Technology, Art, etc. Grammatical accuracy is not downplayed and is encouraged with the same rigour and consistency as the teacher continues to judiciously select and sequence material when planning to ensure that the teaching objectives are attainable. The 'incidents' may be examples for the teacher to prompt pupils and to provide opportunities for them to develop the Storyline. These clearly need to be commensurate with the linguistic levels of the pupils involved. For example, in the Storyline, 'Unsere Schule' (see Figure 7.1), the pupils are responsible for creating the characters who attend, decide on the incidents leading up to the open evening, the visiting judge and the final outcome.

The teacher provides the outline of the Storyline and plans the skills practice bearing in mind the cognitive challenge inherent in the tasks prepared. Decisions will be based on the time available, i.e. the number of lessons; the organisation of the pupils, i.e. whole class/pair/group/individual work; the lexis and structures to be taught, practised or recycled; the coursebook and other resources. However, through 'choice' – for example, the characters and incidents created and the use of 'key questions' – pupils are given some ownership of their learning. Monitoring pupils' work during the Storyline is not unlike the monitoring deployed in more traditional approaches where the teacher takes the lead and facilitates at different stages of the lesson. The competent use of dictionaries is crucial and pupils are encouraged to make use of, add to, create and refer to their own wordbanks as they progress through the Storyline. Whilst a number of formative assessment opportunities are possible, there is no reason why a Storyline cannot be used for summative and peer assessment purposes. Figure 7.1 is a suggested Storyline presented as an end-of-unit activity.

Imagination and creativity permeate most of the work covered in MFL and the most successful lessons are those which integrate a number of activities and exercises to develop the different skills and which are carefully chosen to build on previous knowledge and understanding (see *Learning to Teach MFL in the Secondary School*, second edition, Routledge). The Storyline approach is an attempt to encompass these aspects and is based on principles of good practice in MFL teaching which not only develop the skills necessary for proficiency in the subject but also seek to integrate and make connections with those practised in the whole curriculum and the wider community, including that of the TL-speaking communities. It is a holistic and multi-skill approach in which no one skill is taught discreetly (see ibid.). It:

- is cross-curricular and includes ICT;
- provides a purposeful and communicative context for foreign language learning;
- is planned and directed by the teacher;
- considers pupils' interests, creativity and imagination as a valuable resource;

Storyline	Key questions	Teacher activity	Pupil activity	Material	Outcome/ assessment	Skill
School subjects	**Warming up:**	Organise revision – 'running dictation' game	Pupils in groups copying	Authentic timetables with school subjects	Complete the timetables given	**Writing** (Listening, Speaking)
	Wann hast du/hat er/sie . . .?	Teacher asks questions	Whole class activity	Flashcards, OHT	Read and respond to questions, gap filling	**Reading** and **Writing** (Listening, Speaking)
	Gefällt dir/ihr/ihm . . .? Wie findest du/findet er/sie . . .?	Facilitates and monitors	Individuals read pupil profiles write profiles	Pupil profiles from another group/ Germany.	Pupils write school profiles for: celebrity, etc. to be displayed	**Reading** and **Writing**

Incident: Enter the 'best school' contest

Storyline	Key questions	Teacher activity	Pupil activity	Material	Outcome/ assessment	Skill
Introduce school pupils	Wo hast du . . .?	Revises questions	Whole class	Outline of school building, characters, dictionaries, directory/list of German, Austrian, etc. names and addresses.	Pupils label school classrooms for subjects to be taught in their school and give reasons. Pupils include new reasons from dictionary research	**Writing**
	Wieviele Schüler gibt es? Wie heissen sie? Wie alt sind sie? Wo wohnen sie? Haben sie Geschwister? Wie heisst d'e Schule?	Provides examples of authentic schools.	Pair work activity/ Whole class activity	Word bank with opinions.		**Reading** and **Writing**
		Brainstorms in TL using mind maps and elicits from pupils personal ID characteristics and opinions	Pupils work in pairs/ groups using dictionaries and wordbanks to create school and characters. They present these using OHP or PowerPoint and display.			
	Wie sind die Lehrer?					
		Uses writing frame for advert – models presented. Facilitates	Pupils write adverts for teaching and other staff in their school (ICT)	Authentic adverts, ICT- digital camera, video, OHP, dictionaries, wordbank, audio tape	Pupils write adverts and prepare possible interview questions.	**Reading and Writing**

Incident: Interview for staff, pupils – unsuitable candidates, etc.

Figure 7.1 Unsere Schule

Storyline	Key questions	Teacher activity	Pupil activity	Material	Outcome/assessment	Skill
Classroom Furniture/Equipment	Was brauchen die Schüler/Lehrer? Welche Möbel gibt es?	Teacher provides catalogues (internet material) with classroom furniture/equipment	Pupils select and order	Internet material or catalogues, dictionaries	Pupils complete order form	**Reading and Writing**
			ICT – furnish classrooms with a description in TL. Present and display	OHTs, paper, PowerPoint	Create classrooms with descriptions and a wordbank of furniture/equipment	
	Was ist neben/gegenüber/in der Mitte von . . .? etc.	Circulates, supports and monitors	Read descriptions and find discrepancies			

Incident: wrong order received, furniture/equipment is stolen on arrival, etc.

Storyline	Key questions	Teacher activity	Pupil activity	Material	Outcome/assessment	Skill
School Open Evening	Warum möchtest du an diese Schule kommen?	Uses writing frame with examples of invitations.	Whole-class activity	Invitations, posters, adverts, newspapers, prospectuses, dictionaries	Pupils create posters and invitations for school open evening for display. Write advert for local paper/report on the school opening. Peer assessment of posters and adverts – accuracy and potential appeal	**Reading and Writing**
		Provides authentic school prospectuses (internet) draws attention to relevant structures and lexis.	Whole-class activity In groups write invitations and create posters (ICT).	Access to ICT		
	Warum ist diese Schule die beste?		Pupils read and highlight new lexis/positive expressions for use later on			
		Facilitates	Using ICT – create school web page with descriptions of the school interior, pupil and personnel profiles.			
		Arbitrator	In groups decide on judges for 'best school' contest to arrive incognito at school.			

Incident: Unconvinced parent, errors on the web-page/invitation/posters, etc. Selecting the judge

Figure 7.1 continued

- involves the learners in creating the stimulus material for future learning and practice;
- develops the research skills necessary for independent foreign language learning;
- caters for the range of pupils' learning styles and abilities;
- builds on the prior and existing knowledge of the pupils;
- creates opportunities for the pupils to take the initiative;
- is flexible and may be used with any phase and topic;
- contributes to pupils' social development and future citizenship in a multicultural society;
- can form part of the assessment process;
- does not create extra work for the teacher.

Activity 7.1

Think back to a topic you have recently completed. What sort of 'incidents' and 'key questions' could you incorporate into your planning and teaching using a Storyline approach?

A SUGGESTED MODEL FOR PLANNING A STORYLINE – WITH A FOCUS ON READING AND WRITING

As pointed out in *Learning to Teach MFL in the Secondary School*, the challenge for MFL teachers is incorporating into lessons suitable materials and activities at appropriate moments. It requires the teacher to be open to a communicative framework within which each skill is developed equally to allow pupils to generate language in an 'authentic' situation and in an independent way as well as demonstrating progression.

The Storyline outlined above exemplifies the notion of bringing reading and writing closer together which seeks to enhance the learning process by engaging the pupils through a variety of tasks to produce personalised language forms that can lead to a feeling of ownership and achievement. The idea is that, having covered the main linguistic structures and lexis within the context of the topic of school, the Storyline could be considered as an end-of-unit activity over a series of lessons. This does not preclude the Storyline being planned and incorporated into teaching and learning activities right from the beginning of the topic. Practitioners have found that it fits easily into a presentation – practice – production framework.

Planning a Storyline involves the following steps:

1   *Choose a theme* – guided by pupils' needs and interests, relevance, schemes of work, course book, National Curriculum requirements, examination specifications, cross-curricular opportunities; for example, using ICT for extended reading material or for drafting or corresponding purposes.

2   *Decide on possible sequences of the Storyline* – beginning, middle, incidents and conclusion; for example, reading and writing activities can feature at each stage (the design of the school, recruitment of staff and pupils, various incidents from the pupils or prompted by the teacher and developed by pupils, the open evening and contest).

3   *Choose an introduction* – text message, story, postcard/letter (pupils' written work), video clip, song, game, etc. (advert followed by the decision to enter the 'Best school' competition).

4   *Be clear about the teaching objectives and learning outcomes* – decide on related key questions that will develop the sequence of the Storyline and encourage activities to support the development of the skills (reading and writing) as well as the learners' ideas. They

should move from simple to more complex question types; for example, *Wann? Wo? Was?* to *Wie? Warum?*

5   *Organise resources* – authentic and accessible material, artefacts, dictionaries, internet, magazines, pupils' written work from previous Storylines/lessons, catalogues, newspapers, dictionaries, wordbank sheets, cut-out characters/magazines with celebrities, pupils' work, etc.

6   *Assess pupils' work and identify the next learning steps* – formative and summative assessment in reading and writing, peer assessment, plenary activities, presentations (written or spoken); highlighting activities, internet research and use of materials, completing order forms, etc. (reading); profiles, invitations, posters, reporting, etc. (writing).

7   *Evaluate* – did using a Storyline make a difference to teaching, learning or both? To what extent did competence in reading/writing improve? How do I know? Indicators: increased confidence and motivation when attempting reading and writing tasks; pupils persevere during tasks; pupil feedback is used to inform future Storyline planning.

READING AND WRITING SKILLS DEVELOPMENT THROUGH STORYLINE

Findings in consecutive OFSTED subject reports have identified lower achievement levels and progress in pupils' extended reading and writing skills development. With the advent of the National Literacy Strategy and the Key Stage 3 MFL Framework, there are numerous opportunities for the MFL teacher to harness and draw on pupils' knowledge and language awareness to good effect in the subject. A Storyline approach seeks to support this further by providing a number of opportunities to integrate and develop each of the four skills. In this chapter, I focus on the development of pupils' reading and writing skills.

Reading

When reading, we generally read for pleasure or for a specific purpose. In MFL classrooms it is usually the latter to the detriment of the former. The complexity of both tasks requires a number of strategies to be taught by the teacher and to be deployed by the learner as part of a gradual, pedagogic process.

Activity 7.2

Have a look at the reading resources in your department or the internet relating to the topic in Activity 7.1 and consider the range of text types provided to develop and extend pupils' reading skills.

How do you teach your learners to approach one of these texts confidently and ensure that they become familiar with the genre?

Choose 2–3 short texts and devise activities that include at least three of the following strategies:

- skimming for gist;
- scanning for information;
- highlighting and noting specific structures, phrases, vocabulary for later use;
- extensive reading for pleasure;
- intensive reading for specific information and accuracy;
- making inferences.

Reading is a skill in its own right and Storyline can help provide the linguistic tools to enable learners to:

- transfer relevant reading skills acquired at Key Stage 2 to their foreign language learning;
- see how sounds are represented in writing;
- develop their awareness of the different conventions in written and spoken language;
- broaden the range of reading material encountered in the MFL classroom and beyond.

Through pair and group work, social construction of meaning is enabled in the classroom where pupils are able to pool their understanding and which allows reading support from peers and the teacher (see Macaro, 2003). Storyline seeks to encourage pupils to use and discuss strategies/concepts which will vary according to the level of the text and the cognitive demands of the task. This will include 'non-authentic', 'quasi authentic' and 'authentic' material.

Writing

First and foremost, writing is a legitimate form of language expression and offers an additional activity which will benefit the learner beyond the foreign language classroom. It reinforces the other skills including literacy and helps learners to memorise language, thereby reducing the retention load on aural memory. It is important as it clarifies the spoken language and, by so doing, it helps pupils to clarify meaning; for example, *je/j'ai*, in French or *den/dem*, in German. Writing focuses the learner's mind on accuracy and on aspects of the target language which are not always immediately apparent in the spoken language but which are evident in the written form; for example, subject and adjectival agreement in French and cases and word order in German. Much of the communication our learners are involved in is written communication such as email, text messaging. However, extended writing in MFL remains an issue.

Performance in writing is hinged very closely on good reading habits. Consequently, an extensive experience of reading is essential in order for pupils to have plenty of models on which they can then build their own writing. As with reading, this is a gradual process. Learners need to be guided and have lots of practice at each stage so that what they eventually produce is largely correct. The Storyline approach reinforces the focus of different genres and draws on the learners' experience as active participants and their knowledge of writing, such as writing frames, to build confidence and give them a sense of achievement in the target language.

Activity 7.3

Using the framework for guided writing below (based on DfES, 2002a) and the texts from Activity 7.2, plan a writing frame with a series of writing activities to introduce one of the following: invitations, narrative, posters, etc.

- Establish clear aims and purpose of the task.
- Provide examples of the genre.
- Explore features of the text – key learning points identified.
- Define the conventions.
- Compose together.
- Provide scaffolding for learners (using material elicited during the joint activity).
- Independent writing without support.

Writing is seen as part of a process where the focus is not solely on the 'finished product' but on the writer as he or she is writing (see Macaro, 2003).

PRINCIPLES WHEN USING STORYLINE

In order to ensure that the above criteria are effective and realistically achieved in the MFL teaching and learning process, the following key principles should be borne in mind:

1   An inclusive learning environment should be created based on high expectations, praise and mutual respect between pupils and towards the teacher. Whilst the teacher will have planned the Storyline outline and setting, it is the pupils who will select and provide the details for the final product.
2   The Storyline outline selected and devised by the teacher should be an integral part of the subject scheme of work and assessment process. It should be clear how the Storyline builds on pupils' prior learning, covers the four skills, develops cultural and language awareness, encourages further progress and makes connections with other curriculum areas, such as geography, ICT.
3   The Storyline may be developed and reinforced through the presentation – practice – production phases of the language lesson or used as an end-of-unit activity. Key questions form the cornerstone of the approach. Therefore, the questioning technique of the teacher should be graded in order to encourage the pupils to share their existing knowledge at a level commensurate with their ability in the target language and set the context for what will be studied within the framework of a story.
4   Activities planned should be purposeful and challenging, enabling the pupils to communicate their ideas using the four skills in the target language, tackle problems, hypothesise, give reasons and opinions and think imaginatively. Pupils should be clear at each stage about the teaching objectives and learning outcomes to be achieved. Accuracy through modelling and correction should be encouraged at all times. A mix of teacher-led and pupil-led activities should be encouraged if pupils are to feel motivated and have ownership of the final product.
5   Finally, the Storyline should be displayed and, where possible, have a culminating event such as a parents' evening, a school assembly or open day.

Activity 7.4

Look at how a topic of your choice is covered in the departmental scheme of work/coursebook. Using the suggested model for planning a Storyline below and the example 'Unsere Schule' in Figure 7.1, complete the following grid.

Storyline	Key questions	Teacher activity	Pupil activity	Material	Outcome/ assessment	Skill

Activity 7.4 *continued*

Storyline	Key questions	Teacher activity	Pupil activity	Material	Outcome/ assessment	Skill

Incident:

What might the key questions and incidents be?

Activity 7.5

How might the foreign language learning experience of your pupils be enhanced using a Storyline approach? Consider the strengths and possible limitations.

_____

_____

SUMMARY

The development of pupils' reading and writing skills are inextricably linked and, as such, need to be approached as part of a principled and gradual process to facilitate progression and independence. Storyline is an attempt to make coherent connections in pupils' learning experiences across the curriculum, which includes reading and writing activities and related strategies, and also to encourage them to draw on their knowledge and understanding of the world in foreign language lessons. From the outset pupils are involved in developing a story through the creation of characters and a series of incidents, culminating in an ending of their choice. Whilst the approach may initially entail the preparation of extra resources as well as more focused planning, findings from the Comenius Creative Dialogues project would suggest that exploring a more integrated model of language teaching can only serve to motivate learners to participate in the language learning process and ultimately raise achievement levels in the subject and beyond.

Chapter 8   Grammar in the modern foreign language classroom

LYNNE MEIRING AND NIGEL NORMAN

Chapter aims

By the end of this chapter you should:

- have an understanding of the context and significance of grammar teaching in the MFL classroom;
- understand the impact of policy on the teaching of grammar;
- be acquainted with some of the key issues and challenges relating to the teaching of grammar;
- be familiar with a sequenced approach to the teaching of grammar;
- be aware of a range of practical applications of grammar teaching.

SETTING THE SCENE

A panda walks into a café. He orders a sandwich, eats it, then draws a gun and fires two shots in the air.

'Why?' asks the confused waiter, as the panda makes towards the exit. The panda produces a badly punctuated wildlife manual and tosses it over his shoulder.

'I'm a panda,' he says, at the door. 'Look it up.'

The waiter turns to the relevant entry and, sure enough, finds an explanation.

'Panda. Large black-and-white bear-like mammal, native to China. Eats, shoots and leaves.'

(Truss, 2003)

- What can be learned from this story about the role of grammar and punctuation?
- What is their relationship with communication?

WHY IS GRAMMAR IMPORTANT?

If vocabulary is the bricks and grammar the mortar, we can build a wall or a garage, a house or a castle. Just as a house without bricks would collapse, so too would it collapse without mortar. The mortar provides the disconnected bricks with meaning and purpose, a different purpose in each case, but the same mortar. Vocabulary without grammar has shape and meaning, but with grammar it has a unique purpose and definition – the user is empowered to build his own edifice with precision, detail, individuality and style. Take for example, the vocabulary items *car, hit, the, bus*. In this raw form, meaning is certainly conveyed. As soon as grammar is applied, the meaning can be changed for our own purposes. Thus, *The car was hit by the bus*, has significantly changed the meaning without adding any new vocabulary, it is the grammar which has achieved this. In addition, grammar has the further advantage of assisting in the learning process by reducing the demands on memory. This is particularly important for the less able and Special Needs pupil, for whom the memory burden demanded by notional–functional syllabuses is considerable.

GRAMMAR: ITS PLACE IN THE TEACHING OF MFL

- The National Curriculum (England and Wales);
- GCSE.

Traditionally, the school curriculum in England and Wales has been largely determined by the requirements of public examinations. The National Curriculum, first introduced in 1988 (DfEE/QCA, 1999; ACCAC/NAW, 2000) represents a further defining feature. A useful starting point in the consideration of grammar teaching would be to establish the place of grammar within the MFL National Curriculum and GCSE examinations.

Activity 8.1

Consult the National Curriculum for England or Wales and the GCSE specifications and track references, both direct and indirect, to grammar.

National Curriculum	GCSE
e.g. Programme of Study 3.4 (ACCAC, 2000): 'pupils should be taught: the grammar of the target language, and how to apply it at a level appropriate to their ability'.	e.g. AQA 2004 Aims, French, Section 5c: 'this specification should encourage candidates to develop knowledge and understanding of the grammar of French, and the ability to apply it'.

- National Literacy Strategy (England);
- Key Stage 3 National Strategy (England).

A further significant development which has influenced the profile of grammar has been the implementation of the National Literacy Strategy in England (DfEE, 1998). This has played an important part in developing progression in language awareness at pre-Key Stage 3 level, with its emphasis on words, sentences and texts. Building on this, the Key Stage 3 National Strategy Framework for teaching MFL shifts the emphasis from the teaching of grammar through topics (predominant in GCSE specifications) to the focus upon the language itself. Of the five strands that constitute the Framework, grammar is clearly embedded in two: words and sentences.

Activity 8.2

Consult the National Framework Strategy www.standards.dfes.gov.uk/keystage3/ 'Sentences': 7S7, 8S7, 9S7.

Trace the grammatical progression from Year 7 to Year 9. What are the implications for teaching?

	7S7	8S7	9S7
Year 7			
Year 8			
Year 9			
Implications for teaching			

KEY ISSUES AND CHALLENGES IN THE TEACHING OF GRAMMAR

- Status of the target language
- Deductive–inductive
- Technical terms
- Conceptual understanding
- Grammar and communication
- Sequenced approach to the teaching of grammar.

Status of the target language

Is it feasible to teach grammar in the target language? If grammar is integral to language teaching, and an optimal use of the target language is desirable, this principle must surely be applied to the teaching of grammar. Yet there is a common perception that grammar is, by virtue of its content, intrinsically difficult for teacher and pupil in the target language. Possible reasons for this are the teachers' own lack of confidence in dealing with specialised vocabulary, and, as we point out elsewhere: 'the conventions of coursebook practice have not been conducive to consistent target language teaching of grammar'. There is, however, a serious risk that if grammar is taught in English, it will be relegated to a 'different special and difficult category . . . [thus] intimidating and impeding progress in learning' (Meiring and Norman, 2001: 64).

It appears, therefore, that it is the language that is causing the difficulty rather than the understanding of the concept. This applies to both teaching and learning. From a teaching perspective there is support available (see Macdonald, 1993), and for the learner understanding can be facilitated through the skilful use of appropriate visuals and other forms of support.

Activity 8.3

Write a simple but brief explanation in your target language for a Year 7 class of the difference between the first, second and third person singular of the present tense of regular verbs.

_____

_____

_____

_____

If you were teaching this to a Year 7 class, suggest ways in which you might support the explanation, in order to remain teaching in the target language.

Stages of explanation	Support strategies

Deductive–inductive

Which comes first: rule or example? The deductive approach is based upon the rule followed by application of the rule in examples; the inductive approach introduces examples first from which the rule emerges. Both approaches have their place in a balanced teaching and learning environment. As early as 1632, Comenius stated: 'Children need to be given many examples and things they can see, and not abstract rules of grammar'. Yet he did not dismiss the contribution of a more explicit approach: 'rules assist and strengthen the knowledge derived from practice' (cited by Hawkins, 1994: 111). Some grammatical points lend themselves more to teacher explanation of the rule, followed by pupils' practice, whilst others would benefit more from presentation of examples by the teacher, with pupils working out the rule for themselves. Further considerations in selecting an approach would be the age and ability of the learners and the time available. Clearly both deductive and inductive approaches should be seen as mutually supportive, and teachers might consider the most appropriate order according to circumstances. As we also state elsewhere: 'pupils should be encouraged to induce rules of grammar themselves from a plethora of examples, and also to express these rules in their own words, which the teacher can then use as a basis for a more formal explanation' (Meiring and Norman, 2001: 63).

Activity 8.4

From the grammar of your target language, categorise *six* grammatical points that pupils would encounter in Key Stage 3. Consider whether the initial encounter with the grammar would be better served by an inductive or deductive teaching approach.

Inductive	Deductive

Consider in each case whether your opinion would change if you were teaching the same points to Key Stage 4 and Sixth Form, or according to the ability level of the class.

_____

_____

_____

_____

Technical terms

The National Literacy Strategy should have raised pupils' awareness of technical terms in their mother tongue, thus providing a basis for teachers to introduce the same concepts in the foreign language. In cases where pupils are not aware of the terms and concepts, this can be an obstacle to learning; where they *are* aware they are able to use dictionaries, glossaries, etc. with greater ease, and progress is thus faster. The key to the use of technical terms is surely to use them in context, where they can be referred directly to the relevant language as it arises, and to avoid gratuitous use of over-complicated terms. The knowledge of technical terms has the potential to enable pupils to categorise new language, which will facilitate future retrieval, recycling and re-use. Pupils of all abilities benefit from this type of 'filing system', so that they can develop an ordered approach to what they learn. As Pachler and Field (2001: 141) note: 'By introducing new linguistic structures through unfamiliar terminology MFL teachers run the risk of their pupils struggling with concepts at a level one step removed from the linguistic phenomenon itself.' And, 'Metalanguage can be introduced once a concept is understood by pupils.'

Activity 8.5

Consult a Key Stage 3 coursebook and list the grammatical terms that pupils are likely to encounter. Find target language equivalents. How many of the terms are cognates?

English term	Example	Target language
e.g. possessive pronoun	*mon, ma, mes*	(pronom) possessif

Conceptual understanding

It is important to establish conceptual understanding of grammar from the early stages of learning a language, a process that could be described as 'concept planting'. It shares many of the characteristics of what has been called 'form-focused instruction', which is any planned or incidental instructional activity that is intended to induce the language learner to pay attention to linguistic form. Pachler and Field (2001: 132) propose a sequence for the staged development of grammatical awareness from 'noticing' to 'integrating' to 'internalising' to 'proceduralising'. Thus learners notice or identify and label the language form, formulate a personal rule, link it to previous knowledge, apply it and use it automatically through regular usage in a range of contexts. The Verb Phrase, for example, demonstrates a complexity of features (e.g. variety of verb forms, tenses), but the principle of concept planting should still apply. Confusion often arises because, in the initial stages of language learning, a unit of words is taught lexically, rather than grammatically; for example, *j'ai douze ans, j'ai un frère*. Pupils need to be taught, and thus show understanding of, the function of *je/j'*, rather than to learn it by heart, as an item of vocabulary. This will enable them to recycle and transfer language in new contexts.

Activity 8.6

Suggest strategies for 'planting' the concept of the following grammatical points at an early stage of learning language. What grammatical points would be made more accessible through knowledge and understanding of gender and tense?

Gender (masc., fem., neuter)	Strategies and techniques for concept planting	Related grammatical points (e.g. prepositions)

Perfect Tense	Strategies and techniques for concept planting	Related grammatical points

Grammar and communication

An unfortunate consequence of the prevalent interpretation of communicative approaches to foreign language teaching has been the polarisation of grammar and communication at opposite ends of the pedagogical spectrum resulting in a marginalisation of grammar. Yet communicative competence consists of four components, the first of which is grammatical competence. The setting of grammar and communicative approaches against one another in the classroom does a disservice to both; each has its place in a balanced approach.

As they stand, communicative syllabuses allow for relatively complex grammatical utterances to be used as chunks of language in phrasebook fashion. Thus, the first lesson of French commonly produces for example '*Comment t'appelles-tu?*', a sentence that involves the question form and reflexive verb form, arguably a complex utterance to grasp structurally. It would be foolish to attempt to analyse the components of the utterance at this stage; however, it is useful to highlight such features as the personal pronoun and verb endings. This provides a starting point for raising awareness of language, which can be built upon subsequently. Turner presents this as 'a spiral staircase . . . which implies that grammatical items will come back round throughout the course. In other words, learners will gradually build up their knowledge of the grammatical system through the revisiting and extension of what has been covered in the past' (1995: 18). In this way, the apparent mismatch between grammar and communication is a perceived rather than an actual difficulty and both elements can be mutually supportive.

Activity 8.7

Consider the sentence '*Je voudrais aller au marché pour acheter un kilo de pommes.*' Identify the separate grammatical features of the sentence, and consider which ones you would emphasise to learners at an early stage to contribute towards raising their awareness of language forms.

Choose another sentence in your target language that contains a range of grammatical features, and analyse it in the same way.

Je voudrais aller au marché pour acheter un kilo de pommes.	Grammatical features (e.g. conditional)
(Your sentence)	

Sequenced approach to the teaching of grammar

As we have established, the importance of a sequenced approach to the teaching of grammar is paramount. The role of the teacher is crucial in making 'a judicious selection of grammatical structures with a high indicator of usefulness and generative potential . . . that will be useful in terms of transfer value' (Jones, J., 2000: 146–7). A significant aspect of this is the recycling of previously acquired concepts. The danger of a topic-based approach is that the grammar will be confined to discrete units, dependent upon the topic content. Thus, at the beginning of each new unit of work a 'brainstorming' of the predicted language would enable the recycling of some items. Pachler and Field (2001: 134) suggest that the selection of grammar should be based upon the following considerations:

- Which items need to be 're-cycled' from previous units covered?
- Which items meaningfully build on existing knowledge?
- Which items should not be explained in full at this stage, but will require revisiting at a later stage?
- Which items can be treated as lexical items at this stage?

In a topic such as shopping, pupils could conceivably determine that they would need to learn expressions of quantity. Such an approach empowers pupils, promotes thinking skills and motivates them through progression. It is important that linguistic recycling and spiralling becomes a practical reality. The four-stage lesson suggested in the Key Stage 3 National Strategy (DfES, 2003b) might well provide a useful platform for the incorporation of more regular and sequenced revisiting of language.

Activity 8.8

Consider the topic of holidays in a Year 9 class under the following headings.

Recycled items	Existing knowledge	Grammatical items requiring explanation	Items to be taught lexically

PRACTICAL APPLICATIONS OF GRAMMAR TEACHING

Clearly the issues raised above demand a range of strategies and resources. An overriding recommendation must be that an integrated approach to grammar is adopted rather than a 'bolt-on' approach in the mother tongue. The following are some examples of possible approaches, ranging from 'high tech'/state-of-the-art to 'no-tech'/no frills.

'High tech':

- The interactive whiteboard allows pupils to manipulate words on screen effortlessly.
- Grammar software and websites enable repeated and individualised practice with instant, non-threatening feedback.
- The use of PowerPoint and interactive software enables the teacher to enhance presentational techniques, using the potential of graphics to clarify concepts.

'No tech':

- Colour-coded cards for the establishment and practice, for example, of gender and agreement.
- Timelines to establish the concept and use of tense.
- 'Washing lines' to illustrate and practise, for example, word order.

Use these suggestions as a basis for further activities. For other practical suggestions see Biriotti (1999), Neather (2003) and Rendall (1998).

Activity 8.9

Following the examples given in this chapter, suggest other techniques and strategies for presenting grammar and helping learners to understand concepts.

'High tech' strategies	'Low tech' strategies

SUMMARY

It will be apparent from the arguments advanced in this chapter that the issue of grammar in foreign language teaching is both contentious and complex. Consideration has to be given to the impact of policy on practice. Nevertheless, teachers retain considerable autonomy in interpreting the demands of the curriculum. Having established in this chapter the importance of grammar, we have tried to suggest a reasoned approach consistent with prevailing communicative methodology. In so doing, we have attempted to address some of the most contentious issues in grammar teaching and shown the potential of an approach based upon recycling of previously acquired concepts. We have also demonstrated that this contributes to the development of language awareness more effectively than a purely topic-based approach. Although we recognise the potential of new technologies in achieving this, much can be achieved through more simple strategies.

The unnatural separation between grammar and communication in the past has clearly militated against a balanced approach to foreign language learning. Integration of the two that recognises the role and potential of both will enable progression and enjoyment.

USEFUL WEBSITES

Really Useful French teaching site
www.btinternet.com/~s.glover/S.Glover/languagesite/Default.htm

Really Useful German site
http://atschool.eduweb.co.uk/haberg/reallyusefulge/default.htm

Quia site
www.quia.com/web

Interactive Activities for French Teachers and Learners
www.zut.org.uk/Home.html

Hot Potatoes software site
http://hotpot.uvic.ca

Linguascope
www.linguascope.com

About French Language
http://french.about.com/od/grammar

Language Guide
www.languageguide.org/francais/grammar

Real French
www.realfrench.net

Tex's French grammar
www.laits.utexas.edu/tex/gr

Chapter 9   Cultural awareness and visits abroad

SHIRLEY LAWES

Chapter aims

By the end of this chapter you will:

- have considered different interpretations of 'cultural awareness';
- have gained some insights as to the value of a cultural dimension in the MFL classroom and how it can be integrated into foreign language learning in an engaging and stimulating way;
- explored some practical ideas for classroom use;
- have considered the potential of various types of visits abroad for promoting cultural knowledge and learning.

WHAT DO WE MEAN BY 'CULTURE'?

There are two ways that we generally understand 'culture'. The first is as 'high culture', or what I will call 'enrichment culture', that is often considered 'elitist' and not relevant to most foreign lanuage learners; the second sees 'culture' in a broader sense, focusing on daily life, customs and traditions which are more relevant and accessible to young people. This is what I will call 'ethno-culture'. I want to argue that these interpretations are not mutually exclusive, but that only through exposure to enrichment culture will learners of foreign languages move beyond their parochial, subjective experiences to appreciate cultural achievements that have spread beyond national boundaries and are part of universal *human* culture. So, yes, it is important for pupils in English secondary schools to know about school life in France, about Italian food, Spanish traditional festivals or German home life, but cultural awareness should not stop there. Nor should enrichment culture be 'saved up' for the minority of pupils who continue studying foreign languages at A/S and A-level on the basis that it is too difficult for younger learners.

Culture, in an ethnographic sense, is relativised. The idea is that there is not one human culture, but many, all distinct, different and unique. Cultural relativism is very influential at the present time and not easy to argue against, when 'difference' and 'identity' rather than common humanity are celebrated. However, there is a danger that the elevation of cultural identity and difference as a way of understanding 'culture' can lead to a reinforcement of stereotypes and barriers between people. MFL, after all, have the unique potential in the school curriculum of overcoming barriers between people and promoting a universal outlook. Cultural awareness in this ethnographic sense, that introduces customs, traditions and aspects of daily life, or ethno-culture, to the foreign language learner, is essential of course, and foreign language learning is often best contextualised in the target culture. But what we should be encouraging young people to see are similarities, rather than differences, and to recognise the superficiality of apparent difference. What often *appears* as 'difference' is entirely superficial. Take, for example, 'school life'. Certainly the pattern of the school day varies from country to country, there may be some differences in the curriculum, but, essentially, schooling has similar functions the world over. Pupils around the world have subjects they like or do not like, they have homework, favourite teachers and social relationships. When foreign language learning opens 'windows on the world' in a such a way that shows young people in one country come to understand that, fundamentally, young people in other countries are not very different, we are teaching them about common humanity.

It is also possible for enrichment culture, by which we mean art, literature, poetry, theatre, music, to promote the idea of common humanity, but in a different way. By exposing young people to the best that humanity has achieved and aspired to, the best that is known and thought, we are perhaps assigning a higher purpose to education. What we are doing is taking areas of knowledge that have traditionally been the preserve of a tiny section of society and reclaiming them for everyone. By introducing young people to the culture of a foreign country through the greatest and most creative works that a society or an individual has achieved, we can inspire them, perhaps not to become great artists or writers or poets, but at least to see that there is more to the foreign language and culture than the functional and sometimes banal representations they normally experience.

HOW DO WE 'DO' IT?

With confidence, enthusiasm and a certain amount of skill! 'Cultural awareness', while being a requirement of the National Curriculum (NC), is often a neglected area in practice. The natural focus of the MFL teacher is on language, and 'cultural awareness' elements in lessons are often ad hoc and incidental. The cultural learning that the NC refers to is of an ethno-cultural nature, although there are some excellent examples from practice of how teachers have used poetry, cinema and literature at Key Stage 3. The potential of enrichment culture both as a discreet aspect of and as a resource for foreign language learning tends to have been largely ignored by policy-makers and writers, for the reasons outlined above. It has been left to creative classroom teachers who have a passion for their subject to recognise the value and potential of this aspect of cultural awareness. Cultural learning of both kinds needs careful planning that is integrated into the planning for foreign language learning.

Activity 9.1

Choose one area in the NC Programme of Study for Key Stage 3, or from the syllabus you are following in school. Now consider how you might integrate cultural learning and knowledge into the unit that you have chosen.

- First, brainstorm ideas about what ethno-culture and enrichment culture could be appropriate.
- From the list you have drawn up, consider which ideas can be integrated into a unit of work (for about a three- to four-week period).
- How could the cultural knowledge contribute to an end of unit piece of group work?

Activity 9.2

From the very early stages it is possible to teach about the geography of the country or countries where a language is spoken. One obvious example is in teaching north, south, east and west. This could be introduced using the OHP or interactive white board. Begin with a clear, simple outline map of the UK and introduce four key towns in England.

- Write a dialogue of the teacher and pupil language that might be used. The next step would be to show an outline map of the target country and introduce four key towns in the same way.
- What further practice activities could follow?
- What pair activity could you use?
- In what ways could you develop this from a cultural perspective? Perhaps using images of the towns? Tourist information websites have images that can be downloaded.

Another topic area could be transport.

- How could you develop pupils' knowledge of the country here?
- What resources could you use?
- How could you develop the theme into looking at other countries where the target language is spoken?

Ethno-cultural awareness

Every topic area within the NC Programme of Study (PoS) offers a range of possibilities for integrating ethno-cultural elements and there are a number of excellent publications devoted to the area (see for example Buchanan, 2002; Jones, B., 1992, 2000; Pachler and Field, 2001; Pachler, 1999; Snow and Byram, 1997). There is an emphasis in the NC PoS on the personal, that is, pupils talking about themselves and their immediate experience: their likes and dislikes, family, home and so on. However, ethno-cultural themes, through a focus on the country or countries where the target language is spoken, move the learner beyond the personal and offer new contexts for the recycling of existing foreign language knowledge and for extending foreign language use, in addition to learning about people and life in other countries. It is possible, over a period of time, to build up stock of ethno-cultural knowledge that builds confidence in the learner and makes foreign countries and peoples seem less 'foreign'.

Enrichment culture

What I have called 'enrichment culture' not only enriches pupils' cultural knowledge and understanding, but also the content of the NC. A common criticism of pupils and teachers alike is that the NC is repetitive and not always very challenging in terms of the topics and the largely transactional nature of the language content. Maintaining pupils' motivation has become a more acute problem now that MFL are no longer compulsory at Key Stage 4. The possibilities are endless for introducing enrichment culture knowledge from the beginning of foreign language learning. At Key Stage 3, works of art, poems and music are perhaps the most accessible.

Activity 9.3

Consider the ways in which paintings can be used to develop cultural knowledge and at the same time act as a resource for foreign language learning. You will need to access the website WebMuseum: www.ibiblio.org/wm/paint.

- Browse through some sections and think about how different types of paintings could be used in the MFL classroom. Paintings offer a variety of opportunities for using descriptive vocabulary.
- Select either the work of one artist or a type of painting (e.g. portraits, landscapes) and think about what structures or vocabulary a single or several paintings could be used to support.
- For the painting(s) selected to have any meaning in terms of enrichment culture you need to go a stage further. A lecture on the 'school' that the paintings come from might not be the most exciting way of doing this! How are you going to pitch the level of background cultural information? You might, at an early stage, keep to one or two items of information, such as the name of the paintings, the painters and their nationality.
- How you develop this theme over a number of lessons?
- How will you ensure that the cultural knowledge that pupils have gained over a period of time is valued as much as the language they have learned in that period?

Access to works of art is relatively simple via the internet and when downloaded and projected on a smart board are very impressive. However, if these facilities are not available, posters and prints are a fairly inexpensive alternative and a durable resource. Equally, for group or pair work, postcard 'books' of many famous painters are readily available in art shops and galleries.

In addition to benefits to pupils, enrichment culture also offers teachers the opportunity of drawing on and sharing their own cultural interests or of developing new ones. Sharing this sort of cultural knowledge is potentially more interesting for the teacher than aspects of everyday life!

TEACHING AND LEARNING RESOURCES

Perhaps one of the factors that has discouraged teachers from fully exploring aspects of ethno-culture is the perception that large amounts of 'authentic' materials and realia are needed. Collecting restaurant menus, timetables, publicity materials and the like is not always easy unless one makes regular trips to the target country. Equally, there is also some scepticism about using 'difficult' texts with learners in school. Most materials, if used creatively, can be used with most learners. It is *how* they are used that is important. As we know, it is not necessary to understand every word of a text in order to pick out key words or phrases, but the use of any authentic text needs careful planning and preparation. In France, the '*bande dessinée*' is an important cultural phenomenon. Pupils can be introduced to some of the most well-known comic strips, and produce their own. TV and film are both excellent media for enhancing ethno-cultural knowledge and bring the country and its people alive for pupils of all ages. One of the most memorable lessons I have observed was a class of Year 9 pupils working on a section from the Tavernier film, *Ça commence aujourd'hui*, a gritty, but realistic depiction of everyday life in northern France. At a later stage, the class went on a visit to Lille and saw another side of life in that part of the country. However, TV and film are sadly the least-used resource in MFL classrooms, even when the technology is readily available, and yet for developing listening skills they can be used in exactly the same way as the conventional tape recorder, and are far more enjoyable.

The richest source of cultural materials is the internet. Of course, the problem here is that the choice is sometimes too great. Perhaps the best starting point is to go into the websites of foreign cultural institutions in England, such as the Institut Français or the Goethe-Institut, which have web pages dedicated to educational and cultural materials. The Association for Language Learning (ALL), the National Centre for Languages (CILT) and the British Council all have links to other foreign language education sites. Many government Ministry of Culture sites now have education sections. New technologies that are increasingly available in schools make it possible to use internet resources much more easily.

VISITS ABROAD

School visits and particularly exchanges abroad have become less of a feature of the broader MFL curriculum in recent years. There are a number of reasons that account for this. Most frequently teachers' increased workload is cited, together with fears about possible litigation in the event of an accident. Without dismissing these reasons, perhaps a more important factor is parents' and, indeed, young peoples' reticence about such trips. Societal influences about the perceived possible dangers and risks involved in staying with an unknown family in a foreign country are prevalent (see Lawes, 2000: 92–4) and have had a damaging effect on school trips in general and those to a foreign country in particular. As a result, foreign language teachers find it increasingly difficult to start up new ventures and we need to recognise that more preparation and 'marketing' is necessary than might have been the case in the past.

A school visit can develop out of, or be the culmination of, cultural awareness work that has gone on over a period in the classroom. Alternatively, it could provide a stimulus for future work in the classroom. Home stay visits need more preparation than other types of visit, particularly given the points made above. Technology allows contacts with school pupils abroad to be well-developed before any visit takes place. Besides email correspondence, it is possible to organise video-conferences so that pupils (and possibly their parents!) can meet 'virtually' before meeting in person. If there is reticence about staying in a family, an alternative could be for groups from both schools to have a joint study trip staying in a residential centre. This offers different possibilities from a home-stay, and can in fact be more successful in both linguistic and cultural terms.

Activity 9.4

You are organising a five-day residential visit to France (Germany, Spain, Italy) for a group of 25 Year 8 pupils. They will be meeting up at a residential centre for schools with a group of similar-aged pupils from the target country. The centre is on the outskirts of a small town in a rural setting, but within reach of the capital city. It is set in a wooded area, with a small outdoor theatre, a classroom area, swimming pool and open space for some sporting facilities (e.g. badminton, volleyball, table tennis, football). Plan an outline programme for the visit to include a strong cultural element as well as a linguistic and social focus.

- Consider first what your aims would be.
- Identify a theme for the programme.

Activity 9.4 *continued*

- Map out an outline programme that includes cultural, linguistic and social activities.
- How could the visit be prepared for in school?
- How would the visit be followed up?

Whatever the type of visit chosen, it is essential to build for it beforehand within class lessons. Such preparation can be done sensitively without excluding anyone who is not taking part. When small numbers of pupils from different classes are involved, the teacher might bring them together on a regular basis, at lunchtimes, for example, to prepare both linguistically, culturally and personally. The benefits that visits abroad can bring to the individual pupil, the foreign language department and the school as a whole far outweigh the perceived difficulties and need to be promoted more actively. For a detailed discussion of visits and trips abroad see *Learning to Teach MFL in the Secondary School*, second edition, Routledge.

SUMMARY

'Cultural awareness', both as ethno-culture and enrichment culture, has great potential in stimulating MFL learning and in general educational terms. At a time when there is a need to promote MFLs within the school curriculum and to encourage pupils to continue MFL study beyond Key Stage 3, enrichment culture offers a 'new' dimension to the subject area. Equally, it offers teachers the opportunity to explore new areas and develop their own creativity.

USEFUL WEBSITES

Fédération internationale des professeurs de français
www.fipf.org

TV5
www.tv5.org

Goethe Institute
www.goethe.de

CILT
www.cilt.org.uk

Association for Language Learning
www.all-languages.org.uk

WebMuseum
www.ibiblio.org

French Foreign Ministry
www.diplomatie/fr/culture/france

Institut Français de Londres
www.institut-francais.org.uk

Instituto Cervantes
www.cervantes.org.uk/

Italian Embassy in London
http://italyembassyhomepage.com/

Chapter 10 Internet-based approaches to modern foreign language teaching and learning

NORBERT PACHLER

Chapter aims

By the end of this chapter you should be aware of some of the benefits of the use of ICT in foreign language teaching and learning by having:

- considered some conceptual and practical considerations of ICT use;
- examined aspects of the potential of collaborative web-based work.

INTRODUCTION

It is widely acknowledged that ICT has an increasingly important role to play in education in general and the teaching and learning of foreign languages in particular. In the space available it is not possible to do justice to the myriad of possibilities stretching from the use of (digital) audio and video recordings, computer-assisted language learning (CALL) software, such as text manipulation programs, to delayed- (asynchronous) and real-time (synchronous) computer-mediated communication such as email, chat and audio- and video-conferencing. In order to be able to go beyond very superficial treatment of the wide-ranging field of ICT tools and applications, I focus here on web-based project- and partner-finding resources as well as on so-called tracks and webquests.

This chapter builds on and deepens aspects of ICT use covered in *Learning to Teach Modern Foreign Languages in the Secondary School* second edition (Pachler and Field, 2001: Chapters 12 (ICT) and 8 (Culture)) with particular reference to the new pedagogical skills required by MFL teachers to develop a range of relevant skills, knowledge and understanding of and about the target language and cultures in order to enhance and enrich students' learning experience.

THE CHANGING ROLE OF THE TEACHER AND LEARNERS AS ACTIVE PARTICIPANTS[1]

The role of the teacher in effective ICT-based foreign language teaching and learning is very important, particularly in the identification of a manageable number of relevant websites, as well as in providing clear tasks and exploitation activities and sufficient preparation of and guidance and structure for students.

Chang (2004: 338–9), in the context of electronic learning environments, sets out guidelines which also seem helpful – with some adaptation – for current purposes.

Roles	Responsibilities	Contributions
Assisting instruction	Respond to students' questions concerning course contents	Provide quickened responses
	Monitor online discussion	Shorten perceived psychological distance
	Provide students extra information for better learning effectiveness	Improve the quality of instruction
	Clarify ambiguity concerning course assignments and grading criteria	
	Keep track of students' attendance	
	Post-routine class announcements	
Initiating social connectedness	Initiate interactions with students	Increase students' support structure
	Provide students with required information	Increase students' level of comfort
	Encourage students and explain the advantages of participation in activities	Shorten perceived psychological distance
	Participate in students' activities	Increase the quality of instruction and learning
	Guide students to their learning goals	
	Provide extra help	
	Contribute own experience or insights to assist interactions	
	Respond to students' concerns	
Provide technical support	Coach students on fundamental skills	Reduce technological difficulties and concerns
	Help students in solving access problems	Increase students' support structure
	Help students in locating specific resources	Increase students' level of comfort
	Refer students to other resources when technological problems are not able to be resolved	Increase learning effectiveness and efficiency

Just as the role of the teacher changes, so does that of the student. Essential to the approach taken in this chapter is a cognitive and interactionist view of learning which does not see students as passive recipients of a transmission and delivery mode of teaching, but instead as active participants. In this paradigm of learning, ICT becomes a powerful tool for discovery-based and problem-orientated learning, allowing students to construct new understandings through ICT-based exploratory activity. Collins and Berge (1996) list a number of important changes for learners, among them the need to construct knowledge rather than receive it, focus on its use, solve problems rather than memorise facts, ask and refine their own questions and search for answers, work independently and autonomously with a wide range of resources, as well as collaboratively with others and in teams.

Evidently there exist a number of similarities to MFL teacher behaviours and interventions in contexts that make little or no use of new technologies and or collaborative approaches. Nevertheless, there are also significant differences not only in the planning and the type of teacher interaction with pupils, but also in its nature, such as the type and speed of feedback.

The provision of technical support and what Chang calls 'initiating social connectedness' clearly pose new challenges to MFL teachers working in technology-enhanced contexts. Also, induction of pupils into collaborative approaches becomes very important in project-orientated approaches to teaching, as pupils cannot simply be expected to possess the complex skills involved. And for the teacher a broader set of classroom and behaviour management issues comes into play.[2] Project-based approaches to knowledge generation go well beyond traditional transmission and delivery models of teaching and include what Bessenyei (2002) calls 'knowledge management': not merely the mediation but also the creation, updating, documentation and distribution of knowledge in groups and teams and in networks within classrooms as well as without, importantly through the use of the internet.

PEDAGOGICAL IMPLICATIONS

A logical pedagogical implication flowing from the above is an increased emphasis on collaboration. Project-based approaches are among other things characterised by the collection, sorting, documenting and categorising of information and through intensive communication, co-operation and process-based reflection.

In *Learning to Teach MFL in the Secondary School* (Pachler and Field, 2001: 158), a number of phases of ICT-based project work are outlined. Bessenyei (2002) notes that project work entails systematic and collective planning from vision to evaluation by students and the teacher. This typically includes the development of joint visions, the clarification of ideas, the articulation of aims, the activation of existing knowledge, awareness raising about issues and themes, the formulation of hypotheses, decision making about choice of topics, tasks and timescales. Collaboration among students but importantly also negotiation by teachers with students are important features. In addition, cross-curricular and interdisciplinary approaches usually yield fruitful results.

Work at the *Staatliche Seminar für schulpraktische Ausbildung Albstadt* (see www.seminar-albstadt.de/semiproj/methode.htm) introduces the notion of 'critical points' which warrant particular attention during the planning phase. Colleagues in Albstadt distinguish four phases of project work and associated indicative critical points. Their model is adapted here.

Structured plan	Indicative critical points
1 Partner and topic finding phase	
Identify a partner or partner class with the help of the internet (see below for possible tools) as well as a common topic, activities and goals.	What topics might have particular resonance in other schools or countries? Is the topic of interest to the entire class? Is it possible to identify a mutually suitable time? How can the danger of teacher dominance be overcome?
2 Planning phase	
Teachers and students jointly structure the project. They: • formulate lead questions • develop a work plan • identify the utility of the project	Problems include: • adequate subject- and ICT-knowledge of students leading to teacher superiority • time and curriculum pressures leading to overambitious project plans
3 Project phase	
Students, guided by the teacher: • seek relevant information • carry out activities and develop artefacts • prepare presentations	Problems can occur with group and team work because of: • unequal division of labour • changing moods • lack of stamina

4 Presentation and evaluation phase	
Students, guided by the teacher: • prepare a display • give a presentation • critically reflect on work carried out in phases 1–3	Potential problems include: • lack of presentation skills and techniques by students • failure to complete tasks; for example, because of lack of time • inability to produce adequate artefact • lack of knowledge about project evaluation • 'death by PowerPoint presentations'

Phase 4 of the above model stresses the importance of evaluation which, unfortunately, is often omitted in the project cycle because of time constraints and/or with erroneous reference to the fact that assessment of students' work offers indirect information about the success of project work. However, the checklist of questions for ICT-based project work below, adapted from Bessenyei (2002: 163), shows that a lot can be learnt from detailed project evaluation:

- Did the project aims and goals engage with the lived reality of students?
- Was account taken of students' personal interests and preferences?
- Were the students' personal experiences and their personal knowledge and skills gain documented and reflected on?
- Did the project have clearly defined aims?
- Was the internet used effectively as an information source as well as a communication and presentation tool?
- Was use made of individual and collective contexts for the categorisation, accommodation and assimilation of information?
- Did students systematically document relevant background information used?
- Did students compare local with global data?
- Is collective knowledge construction in evidence?
- Is the project part of a network of similar projects?
- Have the outcomes genuinely been produced by students[3] and do they reflect their personal experiences?
- Are the students required to relate their personal experiences to background information?
- Does the project outcome / artefact communicate a clear message which is appropriate for the target audience?

WEB-BASED PROJECT- AND PARTNER-FINDING TOOLS

A first step towards web-based project work could be the introduction of electronic penpals. *Learning to Teach MFL in the Secondary School*, for example, provides some practical advice in the form of a case study on the use of email partnerships in preparation for a visit abroad (Pachler and Field, 2001: 271–2).

A number of useful websites exist to facilitate email contacts and project work between students and classes. In this way, teachers enable students to engage in authentic communication in the target language and, thereby, they develop their social, linguistic and intercultural competence.

One very popular website is 'Epals.com – Classroom exchange' at www.epals.com. Epals, a multi-lingual online environment, supports project work by enabling teachers and students to search for individual partners, partner classes or partner schools and to promote projects. The website also offers various projects, resources and tools such as monitored email to ensure student safety, multi-functional webmail, discussion boards, online translation or e-cards. One featured project is the Epals bookclub, which allows teachers to find partner book clubs around the world or to share tips and ideas, and it allows students to read book reviews and summaries and post their own or to discuss books with peers.

Another online resource is *The Global Gateway* at www.globalgateway.org.uk/, a free resource from the British Council for schools and colleges seeking international links. Teachers can search for details of schools worldwide and register their own school and project details. They can also access information on how to develop an international dimension in education.

A relatively new scheme, supported by the e-learning programme of the European Union, which aims to put schools in touch with each other, is *eTwinning* at www.etwinning.net. This website allows users to search for partner schools and provides facilities for collaborative work. In addition, the site features practical ideas about themes and scenarios as well as models.

Also there is Tandem Language Learning, a web-based service available at www.slf.ruhr-uni-bochum.de/schools/schools-eng.html. Through the Tandem server, teachers can introduce their students to peers for collaborative partner and project work. Among many other resources, the server offers teacher guides and proposals for activities as well as the results of the European Union funded LINGUA-D project 'Tandem Language Learning Partnerships for Schools', in which over 20 schools and teacher training institutions from France, Germany, Great Britain, Italy and Spain took part from 1998–2000.

A further interesting web-resource in German provided by the Goethe-Institut Moscow is called *Odyssee*. It is available at www.goethe.de/ull/pro/odyssee/. The aim of the resource is to discover other countries by three to four classes sending each other emails once per week for a month. During the first three weeks, students do not know where in the world their partner classes live and each class has a code name. Also, the themes are pre-determined and the students' task is to find out, on the basis of the information contained in the emails they receive, where they are sent from. In the final week any unanswered questions are resolved and the project is evaluated. The project requires students to write, read and discuss in the target language. The website offers a teacher's guide and a workbook for students which contain guidance and specific tasks. In addition, it offers a partner-finding facility.

Activity 10.1

First, familiarise yourself with the functionality of *Epals, The Global Gateway, eTwinning* and *Tandem*.

Then, draw up a list of criteria for a project that might fit into the scheme of work for one of the classes you teach.

Finally, identify a suitable project from those featured on the above sites.

TRACKS AND WEBQUESTS

One popular ICT-based approach which builds on traditional treasure-hunt activities (see e.g. *Finding out about Fontainebleau* in Pachler and Field, 2001: 171–2) are so-called tracks and webquests, discovery-orientated activities in which learners use information found on the internet (see e.g. Mittergeber, 2004). The teacher, through so-called tracks and/or webquest generators (see below), provides clear parameters and a web-based activity structure including learning outcomes, tasks and links to relevant websites. In so doing, the teacher tackles one of the key challenges of the use of the internet in foreign language teaching and learning – information overload and the waste of valuable learning time for aimless searching – and provides a clear path through the wealth of resources potentially available online.

Needless to say, tracks and webquests are not a way for the teacher to side-step lesson preparation and planning and let the learners 'do all the hard work', as their effective use, among other things but arguably most importantly, necessitates the identification of websites that possess what can be called maximum 'affordances' for the topic under investigation. That is, they constitute a rich information and data source with ample potential for exploitation and knowledge generation and construction. For guiding questions concerning the selection and evaluation of websites for foreign language teaching, see Pachler and Field (2001: 273–4).

In a useful online article available from the webquest website *Ozline* (www.tommarch. com/learning), Tom March (1998), attempting to establish a clear conceptual understanding of the internet and how it can support student learning, tackles three myths of the web – that it is the world's biggest encyclopaedia, an information superhighway and full of useless junk. The question 'Why webquests?' March answers by stressing their affordances in relation to:

- posing questions that honestly need answering, and making available real resources and thereby offering motivation and authenticity;
- providing scaffolding and stepping students through thinking processes typically used by expert learners;
- facilitating co-operative learning in the context of large, complex and/or controversial topics.

In approaching the development of a webquest, the teacher can be seen to have three basic pedagogical options (also see Mittergeber, 2004):

- A problem resolution- or quiz-based format, in which learners have to search for answers to pre-determined questions.
- A product-orientated approach, in which pupils work towards a tangible outcome mostly in the form of an artefact; for example, a webpage, a portfolio, a presentation.
- A process-orientated approach, which involves learners in formulating their own questions and/or in developing points of view and positions in relation to complex subject matter.

A huge selection of webquests and materials is available at www.webquest.sdsu.edu. For more detailed information about the nature and pedagogical implications of webquests see the various articles and writings at www.tommarch.com/writings.

Activity 10.2

Explore the range of webquests available on the *WebQuest* website (www. webquest.sdsu.edu). You might like to start with the ones labelled 'Top' which are deemed by members of the *WebQuest* team to be good examples of the *WebQuest* model.

If necessary adapt it for use with one of your classes.

Finally, evaluate the *WebQuest* with reference to the evaluation questions listed earlier in this chapter.

ONLINE TOOLS FOR TRACKS AND QUESTS

At their most basic, tracks and webquests consist of a few, carefully selected websites with associated comprehension and/or exploitation questions. These can be made available to students on paper, but the inherent danger of this approach is waste of valuable lesson time because of pupils' mistyping of often unintuitive URLs. This 'critical point' can easily be overcome by the use of online templates through which teachers can make 'worksheets' available electronically without requiring any web-editing skills. One other distinct advantage of using such tools is that, by remembering one weblink, the teacher can make resources available to students irrespective of which computer room a lesson may take place in and students can also revisit and follow-up work carried out in class at home.

One freely available tool that allows users to collect bookmarks online is called *My Bookmarks* and is available at www.mybookmarks.com. This internet service allows users to keep browser bookmarks and favorites online so they can access them from anywhere.

Two popular tools offering templates for the design of more complex tracks and webquests by completing online forms without requiring web-authoring skills are *TrackStar* (http://trackstar.4teachers.org/trackstar) and *WebQuest Generator* (www.teach-nology.com/web_tools/web_quest). These simply require users to collect websites, enter them into the online templates and add any annotations for students to guide them through a process of inquiry whereby they may complete a series of tasks that lead to a conclusion or result in a product/artefact.

Activity 10.3

Work through the 'Ten Stages of working the web for education' at www.tommarch.com/writings/ 10stages.php by Tom March. They are intended to provide a set of milestones for teachers using the web with students.

SUMMARY

In this chapter I have introduced a number of online tools and resources which enable MFL teachers to adopt effective collaborative and project-based approaches using new technologies which do not require specific technical pre-requisites either on the part of teacher or learner.

NOTES

1 *Learning to Teach using ICT in The Secondary School* (Leask and Pachler 2005: Chapter 13 (Theories of Learning and ICT)) discusses the nature of the changes to the role of the teacher in more detail.
2 For support and guidance on behaviour management in 'traditional' contexts see for example www.behaviour4learning.ac.uk.
3 *Learning to Teach using ICT in The Secondary School* (Leask and Pachler 2005: Chapter 9 (ICT and assessment)) discusses the issue of plagiarism.

Part 3   Broadening your perspective

Chapter 11 KS2–KS3 transfer

MARILYN HUNT

Chapter aims

By the end of this chapter you should:

- understand the primary modern foreign language (PMFL) context;
- have considered the value of PMFL learning and potential difficulties in its introduction nationally;
- have acquired some ideas for adapting good practice appropriate for teaching MFL to primary learners;
- have gained some insight into transition issues and the practicalities of receiving pupils with prior MFL learning in secondary school.

THE PRIMARY MFL CONTEXT

It was tricky French in Reception . . . we thought we were doing normal work and then we found out it was French!

(Kirsty, Year 1)

This is an exciting and challenging time for foreign languages in the primary sector. Although there has never been a UK-wide policy for PMFL provision, various initiatives and projects have gained momentum and recent government documents relating to England (*14–19 extending opportunities, raising standards*; www.dfes.gov.uk/14–19greenpaper) outlined an entitlement for all primary school children in England to learn at least one foreign language throughout KS2 by 2012. The National Languages Strategy (DfES, 2002a) shortened this time-scale to 2010 and the DfES provided additional funding from 2003–05 for 19 LEA-led Pathfinder projects to identify sustainable and replicable models.

The government's decision to shift the focus of compulsory language learning from 11–16 to 7–14, represents a significant new challenge for primary and secondary schools in England. This radical policy shift started in 1999 by supporting the early language learning initiative to promote and develop PMFL provision with specific actions to create the Centre for Information on Language Teaching and Research (CILT) Good Practice Project with projects across England and Wales and the establishment of a National Advisory Centre for Early Language Learning (NACELL; www.nacell.org.uk). MFL is not statutory in Key Stages 1 and 2, although non-statutory guidelines were introduced in the National Curriculum for

England (DfEE/QCA, 1999). Consequently, staff, training and resources are variable and patchy, but projects and schemes are growing steadily. A QCA research project (Powell *et al.*, 2001) evaluating current PMFL provision indicated 21 per cent of maintained schools with KS2 pupils were offering some form of MFL teaching. A more recent survey (Driscoll *et al.*, 2004) established 44 per cent of schools teaching KS2 pupils offered some form of MFL, but only 3 per cent to all four years.

Schemes include language 'encounters' or languages 'tasters', languages taught in after-school (often commercial) clubs, language awareness programmes in varying guises, and languages (mainly French) fully integrated into the curriculum. MFL KS1 and KS2 provision varies considerably both within and across regions in time allocation (from 5 minutes a day to 120 minutes a week), the MFL starting year (from Year 1 to Year 6), class size and teacher expertise (subject specialist, generalist primary teacher). MFL provision often reflects LEA commitment to promoting MFL in primary schools or individual headteachers who view MFL as a curriculum priority. Recently provision has been extended by the growing number of specialist language colleges as part of their outreach activities for primary schools.

Expert opinion over the efficacy of an early start is divided. The critical period hypothesis has given birth to the 'younger the better' claim that young children have a special instinctive capacity including both speech and morpho-syntactic development and that they can acquire L2 in similar ways to their mother tongue. Yet, research has been at pains to prove that primary time is more productive than secondary time or even that additional primary time guarantees higher outcomes.

Activity 11.1

1 List your arguments for introducing MFL into primary schools. Compare this with the NC guidelines.

_____

_____

_____

2 What issues are entailed in introducing PMFL nationally? What are your views as a secondary MFL school teacher?

_____

_____

3 Consider the local issues relevant to the introduction of PMFL.

_____

_____

The contribution of modern foreign languages to the primary school curriculum

- a valuable, educational, social and cultural experience for all pupils;
- develops communication and literacy skills;

Activity 11.1 *continued*

- exploits differences and similarities between the foreign language and English;
- prepares for life in a multi-lingual and multi-cultural world;
- can develop cross-curricular links.

(Adapted from DfEE/QCA, 1999: 32)

Issues

- What are the implications for teacher supply?
- Who (exactly) will teach languages in primary schools? Specialists visiting schools? Specialists based in school? Class teachers with minimal/some language knowledge? Foreign language assistants with no teacher training?
- Teachers' knowledge/qualifications. How competent are primary teachers expected to be in terms of linguistic / MFL pedagogic knowledge?
- Funding: to allow realistic planning and implementation strategies; to train existing primary staff to become increasingly confident and self-sufficient in language teaching; for specialist PMFL initial teacher training; for pedagogy training for primary/secondary teachers teaching at KS2 and for secondary teachers receiving KS2 pupils with diverse MFL experience; for resources.
- Curricular issues: time/space, which language(s), when . . . How is progression maintained? All four skills? Lessons taught in the target language? Language awareness rather than a specific language?
- The connection between primary/secondary languages curriculum? Links between the KS2/KS3 frameworks?
- Continuity (or otherwise).
- Need for more systematic cross-phase liaison?

SECONDARY TEACHERS WORKING WITH PRIMARY SCHOOLS

Frequently, secondary specialists are asked to work with primary school pupils. In this context, it is important to devise activities appropriate to the pupils' age and development and to ensure materials are matched to both the age and the maturity of the learners and their linguistic competence. Liaison with the classroom teacher would help to discover pupils' developmental stage in reading, writing, number work, etc. It might even be possible to link MFL work with other curricular areas.

The KS2 scheme of work (French (DfEE/QCA, 1999); German, Spanish (DfES/QCA, 2004); www.standards.dfes.gov.uk/schemes3) designed to support teachers of PMFL, provides a framework to help schools develop or adapt their own schemes. Materials are optional and meant to be used flexibly. The scheme includes 12 units and provides information about:

- links with other curriculum areas;
- work at home and outside lessons;
- ideas for listening, speaking, reading, writing;
- teaching and learning approaches; for example, presentation, practice, production; practising new language; ICT.

The KS2 Framework (DfES, 2005b; www.standards.dfes.gov.uk/primary/publications/languages/framework) makes languages an integral part of the primary curriculum and includes five strands – oracy, literacy, knowledge about language, language-learning strategies and intercultural understanding – with learning objectives for MFL in all four years of KS2, as well as advice on introducing languages into the primary curriculum.

Activity 11.2

1   What would you need to consider if you were involved in teaching MFL in primary schools?
2   Look at one unit of the KS2 scheme of work and compare this with your knowledge of what is currently taught in Year 7.
3   Explore the KS2 Framework and consider the implications for KS3.

Suggestions

- Policy and guidelines for KS2 languages;
- Scheme of work;
- Methodology: oral/aural based (see CILT's Young Pathfinder series);
- Seek advice from primary school staff about working with primary children;
- Learning objectives (linguistic and communicative);
- Appropriate resources;
- Assessment;
- Continuity: scheme of work and pupils' MFL records to secondary school.

ADAPTING GOOD PRACTICE FOR KS2

I like it when we can make jokes in French, like: Je mange un hamster.

(Alice, Year 6)

Many basic principles and techniques used at secondary level are readily adaptable to Key Stage 2 with appropriate content and materials. Traditionally at primary level the emphasis has been on speaking and listening, whereas at secondary level equal importance is given to all four skills. Johnstone (1994) suggests adopting a more rounded and integrative approach by preparing primary pupils to work in all skills from the start:

> Fire on all four cylinders. Not only can reading and writing be introduced successfully, but the four modes can reinforce each other, particularly once literacy in the first language has been established.

CILT Young Pathfinder 5 (Skarbek, 1998) includes many excellent ideas for personal and creative writing. Planning for progression is important at all stages of learning. Learning isolated items of language is unhelpful: pupils need to make links in order to start to understand how language fits together and gradually develop the ability to generate their own language in a variety of situations. Language learning skills are also useful to transfer to future learning of other languages.

Activity 11.3

Which elements of good practice at Key Stage 3 are adaptable for Key Stage 2? Complete your own list before comparing with the suggestions below.

_____

_____

_____

_____

_____

Suggestions

- Visuals help to memorise words, focus children's attention and help avoid the use of English. Word flashcards encourage children to link the sound and written word from an early stage. Techniques and games for using visuals at Key Stage 3 are equally suitable for practising language at Key Stage 2; for example, flashcard/OHT/ visual projected on whiteboard (hide and guess, quick flash, slow reveal, hunt the flashcard, hit the flashcard, number the flashcard, memory games, what's missing?, keyhole technique).
- Using realia and authentic materials can be provoking, intriguing and motivating. Objects to handle or pass around help children link new words with the objects, for example food/drink, clothes, or a fake microphone to encourage speaking.
- Presentation of vocabulary using a range of repetition (loud/soft, fast/slow, high/low pitch, talking like robots, etc.) in chorus, groups and then individually to build up confidence. Mime, gesture, actions to present new language.
- Games provide variety and fun but also contain a mechanism whereby pupils repeat again and again, with some variations, the structure to be practised.
- Short-term achievable targets and strategies to help meet these.
- ICT: use of the interactive whiteboard captures pupils' attention and provides active involvement moving images/words. Software presents the opportunity for individualised work where pupils match sound, image and word, and websites appropriate for young learners (see bibliography) provide more stimulating visual appeal than a worksheet or page.
- Kinaesthetic learning through movement, mime, making sentences from individual cut-out words, etc.
- Whole-class participation responding using mini whiteboard or laminated cards with ✔ or ✘.
- Variety of whole-class, pair and group work.

Activity 11.4

I thought French would be boring – all writing – but the teacher makes it fun with lots of different games.

(James, Year 5)

Activity 11.4 *continued*

To extend the repertoire of appropriate activities, think of primary style activities which can be adapted to MFL learning. Compose your list before looking at some suggestions below.

_____

_____

_____

_____

Suggestions

- Use of puppets/soft toy or animal/paper plate mask for role plays.
- Display: washing line and pegs to display vocabulary; alphabet frieze and sound banks of similar sounding words; mobiles with classroom phrases; calendar and weather board; birthday poster; labels around classroom and school.
- Story telling; using stories with repetitive phrases for building up vocabulary and structures; for example, 'The enormous turnip', or familiar stories like 'The Hungry Caterpillar'; use of the 'big book'.
- Active learning; singing, clapping to rhythm of words. These activities, familiar from pre-school groups and current work, help develop more accurate pronunciation, help to reinforce gender, syntax and sophisticated language structures 'painlessly' and allow children to reproduce language with confidence and fluency. Young Pathfinder 6 includes finger rhymes, activity rhymes/songs, and ideas for using familiar tunes.
- Building on literacy work: focus on acquisition of language-learning skills.
- Games and materials used for number and language in English adapted for MFL.
- Links with schools abroad, using videos, email, video-conferencing, visits.

For examples of good practice refer also to the school spotlights DfES website (Driscoll *et al.*, 2004) and the CILT Good Practice website.

CONTINUITY: KS2–3 TRANSITION

Ever-increasing numbers of pupils will enter secondary school with prior MFL learning. This may present a real challenge for secondary MFL teachers confronted with pupils from a range of feeder primary schools where 'entitlement' allows variety in language provision in time allocation, teaching quality (both subject knowledge and pedagogic expertise) and, indeed, the language studied. Good continuity in learning, meaning that pupils should not repeat what they have already learned or have to attempt over-challenging work, both of which could have a damaging effect on pupil motivation, is a real issue in these circumstances. Even in the Scottish initiative, firmly based in the 5–14 curricular context, teachers did not necessarily build on prior learning (Low *et al.*, 1995). Pupils often experienced a change from a relatively open framework, allowing for creativity, to teachers constrained by coursebook-dictated structure.

Many local projects are designed around clusters of secondary and primary feeder schools where joint cross-phase planning of MFL learning leads to a secondary programme building on KS2 achievements. However, as this may not always be possible, effective transition arrangements with prior language learning information to accompany the national common transfer file would assist secondary schools in ensuring secondary teachers are aware of the skills each new cohort brings. The European Language Portfolio (www.nacell.org.uk/ resources/pub_cilt/portfolio.htm) is an open-ended record of a pupil's achievements and detailed progress in languages. It includes details of languages known, learned, where used and favourite activities, as well as a self-assessment record of what a pupil can do in listening, speaking, reading and writing with space for examples of work. Whilst this may be motivational for pupils, it is difficult to imagine how secondary teachers would have time to access all this information. A more streamlined record, compiled by the primary teacher, including reliable information about language work, language skills and language-learning skills covered, and some level of assessment would certainly assist in planning and differentiating in the secondary classroom.

The National Languages Strategy asserts that by age 11 pupils should have the opportunity to reach a recognised level of competence in MFL to be recognised through a national scheme, the Languages Ladder (www.dfes.gov.uk/languages/DSP_languagesladder.cfm), which starts with a basic grade of competence for new learners. Secondary teachers would need to take account of this external assessment if applied at the end of KS2.

As PMFL progresses, it will be necessary to re-think the MFL KS3 curriculum, initially to ensure differentiation, possibly through setting and fast-tracking for early GCSE entry and later to develop curriculum content.

KS2–3 transfer (not mentioned in Pachler and Field (2001) as at the time of publication it was not a serious issue) is currently a topic of major importance and will continue to be so over the next decade whilst changes develop. Readers can imagine how these recent policy decisions create a challenging and problematic scenario for language teaching in both KS2 and KS3.

Activity 11.5

Consider what steps you could take to ensure a smooth transition to secondary school if you are receiving pupils with prior MFL learning.

Suggestions

- Find out:

    - which pupils learned MFL (and which language);
    - topics, vocabulary, skills taught;
    - pupils' attainment;
    - time allocation, teacher competence, etc.

- Departments use this information in planning for differentiation to challenge all pupils.
- Cross-phase liaison to enhance information transfer.
- Reciprocal visits and mutual observation of classes would be valuable in establishing both complementary methodology and continuity, building on content and skills, to value prior learning.
- Pupils visit secondary school for a languages day as part of their induction. They participate in a carousel of language activities or, perhaps more ambitiously, enter France through the '*contrôle des passeports*' with a passport prepared at primary school, change money at '*la banque*', and order products in the café or shops.

SUMMARY

Many primary schools have embraced MFL enthusiastically and recognise its positive contribution to pupils' general development and intercultural understanding. However, concerns remain about staffing, training and funding and even where positive attitudes exist there seems to be some reluctance to assess pupils. The government is keen that PMFL should be fun but should also involve sustained language learning. There is an implicit expectation that PMFL will improve both take-up and results at KS4. The diversity of PMFL entitlement has huge implications for the secondary phase and secondary MFL teachers face a challenging time in reshaping the KS3 curriculum to gain higher outcomes.

USEFUL WEBSITES

KS2 MFL research

www.dfes.gov.uk/languages/DSP_sub.cfm?sub_id=5&cn_pagename=primary&area_id=3

KS2 MFL information

Reports on MFL in primary schools

www.qca.org.uk/ca/subjects/mfl/prim_schools.asp

www.cilt.org/projects/goodprac.htm

www.dfes.gov.uk/languages/DSP_sub.cfm?sub_id=4&cn_pagename=primary&area_id=3
  (KS2 Pathfinder LEAs)

www.des.gov.uk/languages/DSP_nationallanguages_activity.cfm (National Languages
  Strategy)

KS2 MFL resources

www.langprim.org

www.bbc.co.uk/schools/primaryfrench/

www.bbc.co.uk/schools/primaryspanish/ BBC Primary French/Spanish (German planned
  for 2005) designed to support non-specialist language teachers

www.language-investigator.co.uk (Coventry LEA website to accompany 'Thinking Through
  Languages' project.)

www.mdlsoft.co.uk (Click on 'Primary French' for links to clipart files/images to support
  DfES Primary French scheme of work.)

Chapter 12   Working with other adults

ANA REDONDO

Chapter aims

By the end of this chapter you should:

- understand recent policy changes in the area of contractual arrangements of the school workforce and their implications for the professional practice of foreign language teachers;
- be able to apply this understanding in their work with support staff, in particular teaching assistants (TAs).

THE POLICY CONTEXT

In 2003, a historic national agreement was reached between government, employers and school workforce unions to implement new models of teaching and learning in response to a perceived need for innovation in the area of contractual arrangements for the school workforce. Unrelenting reform and innovation – October 2005 saw the publication of the twelfth (!) education White Paper of the Labour Government since 1997 – brings with it increasing pressure on teachers' time resulting from non-teaching activities and the need for reducing excessive workloads (see DfES *et al.*, 2003). These laudable aims, which go hand in hand with other fundamental changes in education policy – notably the Children's Act and the government's five-year plan for education (DfES, 2004) – necessitate the need for remodelling the workforce with wide-ranging implications for teaching and non-teaching staff. Under the so-called remodelling agenda, support staff see their roles expanded and they are increasingly recognised for the contribution they make to the education of young people, be it in their capacity as administrative, technical or, most importantly for our present discussion, as classroom support staff. For teachers this means an aspiration that they should not routinely do administrative and clerical tasks and have support so that they can focus on teaching and learning. By implication, support staff are being asked to take on an increasing range of duties and responsibilities. For both parties these changes in the conceptualisation of their roles and responsibilities make closer collaboration necessary. The DfES *Five-Year Strategy for Children and Learners* (DfES, 2004) sets out the following five strategies for systemic transformation of children's services, education and training:

- greater personalisation and choice, with the wishes and needs of children's services, parents and learners centre-stage;

- opening up services to new and different providers and ways of delivering services;
- freedom and independence for frontline headteachers, governors and managers with clear simple accountabilities and more secure streamlined funding arrangements;
- a major commitment to staff development with high-quality support and training to improve assessment, care and teaching;
- partnerships with parents, employers, volunteers and voluntary organisations to maximise the life chances of children, young people and adults.

The significant changes which flow from these aspirations to the way in which teachers' roles and responsibilities are conceptualised and how they are expected to operate are being addressed through a new set of professional standards for Qualified Teacher Status (QTS), at the time of writing under consultation (see www.tda.gov.uk/teachers/currentconsultations/professionalstandards.aspx). Significantly, the review of the standards is seen by the Teacher Development Agency for Schools (TDA; formerly TTA) as an opportunity to evaluate whether the *Common Core of Skills and Knowledge for the Children's Workforce* (DfES, 2005a) is reflected appropriately in the current standards. The common core, which works from the premise that everyone working with children, young people and families should have a common set of skills and knowledge, sets out the following six areas of expertise (DfES, 2005a: 4) expected from teachers operating in a highly networked environment:

- effective communication and engagement;
- child and young person development;
- safeguarding and promoting the welfare of the child;
- supporting transitions;
- multi-agency work;
- sharing information.

The government has developed a specific set of standards (see www.hlta.gov.uk and www.teachernet.gov.uk/remodelling) for what are called Higher Level Teaching Assistants (HLTA), and HLTA status is awarded by the TDA to those members of support staff who successfully demonstrate that they have met them, with places on the scheme being limited. As a foreign language teacher you need to familiarise yourself with these standards in order to be clear about the roles and responsibilities of support staff and how you can best collaborate with them.

Activity 12.1

Defining roles and responsibilities of teachers and support staff is an important first step in engaging with the remodelling agenda. You can do this, for example, by familiarising yourself with the HLTA standards at www.hlta.gov.uk and DfES guidance (DfES, 2000).

Consider the following questions:

- How do you think pupils' learning can be maximised by the presence of a TA in your foreign language lessons?
- What expectations do you have of a TA's presence in your lesson? What would you expect in terms of his/her contribution?
- How would you consider involving him/her?
- What expertise would you expect him/her to have?

Activity 12.1 *continued*

List the respective responsibilities you think TAs can carry out in foreign language education and how you can best support them in discharging them. It might be helpful to use the following four categories to structure your deliberations:

- support for the pupil;
- support for the teacher;
- support for the curriculum;
- support for the school.

In this chapter we explore the implications of these important changes for foreign language teachers.

FROM POLICY TO PRACTICE

For foreign language educators the issues involved in working with other adults in the classroom are far from new and ostensibly provide an opportunity to consolidate existing practice going on in many classrooms up and down the country who have benefited from Foreign Language Assistants for some time (since 1905 in the UK in fact) and other native speakers routinely deployed in order to bring pupils in closer contact with the target language and culture and its speakers. (For specific guidance on working with Foreign Language Assistants see e.g. Chapter 8 in *Learning to Teach MFL in the Secondary School*, second edition, Routledge or NALA/Central Bureau, 1992.)

Teaching assistants either work with a whole class or support individual or small groups of children. In secondary schools, teaching assistants have traditionally tended to work as special needs assistants supporting pupils with learning difficulties. Under the HLTA scheme, assistants are increasingly working as specialists for a subject and contribute to lesson planning, the development of support materials or class supervision duties.

The activities of this chapter focus on working with other support staff, in particular teaching assistants, through a range of practical activities in the areas of planning (Activity 12.2), lesson evaluation (Activity 12.3), behaviour management (Activity 12.4), assessment (Activity 12.5) and, of course, professional development (Activity 12.6).

Activity 12.2

Imagine you teach a class of 30 mixed ability Year 9 pupils. You have included three activities with several tasks to be completed within each of these in your lesson plan ranging from simple to more complex. The lesson lasts for one hour in which pupils will get a chance to practise speaking, listening and responding and reading comprehension. A TA usually attends your lessons with this group.

Here are a series of questions for you to consider.

How would you approach your lesson? Will you ask the TA to support one or more pupils taking his own initiative? Will you talk to him/her about the activities that will take place in the lesson? If so, when will you do so and why? Will you hand out a lesson plan with specific instructions and guidelines? What are the relative advantages of these approaches?

Activity 12.2 *continued*

Do you think that the TA would immediately understand the purpose of the different activities you are intending to carry out in your lesson? Would he/she be able to predict and support how the learners are going to approach and carry out the tasks? Should you be planning lessons together? What are the advantages and possible constraints?

Is it essential that the TA is familiar with and understands well the outcomes you want to achieve? If so, how would you find out that the TA actually understands the outcomes you are trying to achieve?

How can you ascertain whether or not a TA is effective at supporting the learners? Is it enough for you to judge by the way you see her or him interacting with one or several pupils in the course of the lesson? What can you do to ensure that the TA's contribution to the lesson is most effective?

Do you consider it valuable to meet with a TA you share lessons with on a regular basis? If so, would you meet during your non-contact time or after school? What do you consider to be the best use of time for these meetings? Order the following items in order of priority for your meetings with the TA:

- ❑ planning time is the best time spent with a TA;
- ❑ teaching the TA the meaning and the pronunciation of the vocabulary to be presented in lessons;
- ❑ coaching the TA on how best to support pupils who will be completing some reading comprehension tasks;
- ❑ asking the TA to prepare a drama activity which a small group will perform to their peers.

Suggestion

As part of a practical approach to joint planning with the TA, the following pro formas for lesson and unit planning might be useful.

UNIT OF WORK/
UNIT PLAN
Teaching group:
Number of lessons in unit: ....
Number of pupils in class : .... SEN:............ EAL:.......... G&T.......... Other:.........

Activity 12.2 *continued*

Unit objectives		
Language content and language learning skills		
Language, grammar, cultural awareness 1 Main activities and tasks incl. ICT 2 Materials, resources and equipment 3 Homework		
Ability grouping to work with TA		
Individual pupil(s) identified to work with TA:		

LESSON PLAN
Teaching group:
Lesson … of … Date: ………………
No. of pupils: ……………… SEN:………… EAL:……… G&T……… Other:………

Activity 12.2 *continued*

	Teacher and TA	Pupils
Lesson objectives Educational objectives Linguistic and language learning objectives ICT objectives		
Lesson content: Language, grammar, cultural awareness		
Activities and tasks (including starter and plenary) 1 2 3 Homework Ability grouping to work with TA: Individual pupil(s) identified to work with TA:		
Materials, resources and equipment needed		

Activity 12.3

Joint lesson evaluations

Would you consider it a useful exercise to ask the TA who shares a lesson with you to feedback his evaluation of the lesson? Would you think it practical to provide him with your feedback in return?

How would it influence your planning for the next lesson(s) and your medium-term planning with the group you both share?

Would you consider it practical and valuable to include in departmental meetings discussions on lesson outcomes where both you and the TA have taken part working as a team?

Activity 12.4

How can your behaviour management strategies take into account any contribution a TA makes to your lessons?

How would you define the role of the TA in disciplining learners in your lessons?

If you thought that the TA had also a role in taking some responsibility for managing and improving behaviour in your lessons, how appropriate would it be to consider the following. The TA:

- giving oral warnings to individual pupils;
- setting detentions for after school which he/she will supervise;
- writing a letter home to parents/carers;
- approaching the pupil's form tutor in order to discuss the child's behaviour in MFL lessons;
- telephoning parents/carers to inform them of the pupil's detention;
- telephoning parents/carers to inform them of their child's poor behaviour;
- discussing with the head of department some steps to follow in order to deal with the poor behaviour of a pupil/pupils in a lesson;
- informing the head of department of the action he has taken after an incident of poor behaviour in a lesson with a copy to the teacher whose lesson the TA was working in.

What actions, if any, do you think are definitely outside the remit of the TA's role and responsibility within the classroom and lessons you both share?

_____

_____

_____

Activity 12.5

Assessment is another key area of work. What contribution can a TA make to it? How appropriate are the statements below? You might wish to discuss them with a colleague. TAs:

- should be assessing pupils' work in a variety of skills;
- could carry out marking exercise books;
- might be helpful in assisting pupils in using bilingual dictionaries;
- can help pupils with learning difficulties to copy the vocabulary in their exercise book and ensure that copying is accurate;
- best work with pupils on a one-to-one basis for error correction and feedback;
- should take pupils outside the lesson to work with them to improve their work;
- should prepare specific assessment tasks for those pupils with learning difficulties whom they support;
- should concentrate on assessing and supporting only those pupils to whom they are assigned, in particular those with learning difficulties;

Activity 12.5 *continued*

- should not carry out any whole-class assessment activities;
- can take the register and make notes in the teacher's mark book.

Activity 12.6

In terms of CPD, consider the following questions:

- What areas of your teaching could be improved by working with TAs in your lesson?

  _____

  _____

- In what way do you think you can play a role in a TA's professional development?

  _____

  _____

THE QUESTION OF LINGUISTIC COMPETENCE

If TAs are to be effective in foreign languages lessons, they need to have some basic competence in the language taught. HLTAs might have a background or basic qualifications in a foreign language. Nevertheless, it is likely that they will benefit from refreshing or further developing their skills and communicative competence in the foreign language in order to have enough language and cultural knowledge to be able to complement the work of the teacher in lessons effectively. It is only right to expect that teaching assistants, in particular HLTAs, should attend some courses which provide them with skills and competences that can make their contribution in school more effective. Language enhancement courses are likely to be available externally but the foreign language department also needs to make sure relevant pedagogical support is available in-house in the same way that many departments provide in-house training and support for foreign language teachers.

Some knowledge of a language by the TA would go a long way towards assisting pupils in their foreign language learning. Together with the requisite basic pedagogical skills it can allow for a real partnership between the teacher and the TA. For instance when activities are set out by the teacher in a lesson and clear instructions are given about how to carry out the tasks in hand, TAs are in a good position to guide and support pupils in a one-to-one situation or in group work activities to carry out and successfully complete the work.

When defining strategies which can help young people learn a foreign language such as memorising, grasping grammatical concepts, practising language, language drills and a whole host of other foreign language tasks, TAs can enable learners to remain focused and on-task and feel they can ask for the help they individually require without having to wait unnecessarily long stretches until the teacher is available to do so.

In an online article (see www.talkingteaching.co.uk/resources/show_resource.cfm?id= 80), John Rice notes that there are no great rules for how to work alongside a TA but that there are some common-sense practices which should help maximise the benefits to be derived from additional adult attention. These include:

- do not feel threatened;
- use the expertise available;
- delegate;
- take time to communicate;
- manage your staff;
- value your TA.

SUMMARY

Foreign language teachers have a long tradition of working with other adults inside and outside the classroom. As mentioned earlier, Foreign Language Assistants have long been a fixture in lessons, and on trips, visits and exchanges Foreign Language teachers are frequently supported by parents, governors and others. In response to the government's workforce remodelling agenda, the number of other adults working with Foreign Language teachers will increase and with it the need to adapt approaches to teaching and learning to maximise the benefits to be derived from them.

USEFUL WEBSITES AND RESOURCES

British Council online guidance for Foreign Language Assistant
    www.languageassistant. co.uk
Centre international d'études pédagogiques online guidance for Foreign Language Assistant
    www.ciep.fr/en/assistantetr
Martin, C. (2003) *The Foreign Language Assistant in the Primary School.* NACELL. Available at:
    www.nacell.org.uk/bestpractice/pdfs/The_foreign_language_assistant.pdf

Chapter 13 Reflective practice through teacher research

MIKE CALVERT

Chapter aims

By the end of this chapter you should:

- appreciate the importance of, and the need for, reflective practice;
- understand how reflection can form part of your personal and professional development;
- have gained some insights into the value of classroom research;
- have acquired some ideas for using research to inform your practice;
- have learnt more about sources of information to inform your practice.

INTRODUCTION

Since you have chosen to read this chapter, you have already identified yourself as someone who a) wants to develop their knowledge and skills whether you are in initial teacher education or already in post in school and b) someone who has chosen not only to read the chapters on aspects of teaching, valuable as they are, but to extend your reading and practice and read a chapter that might impact on your development as a teacher overall.

This chapter will set out what reflective practice is, explain how important it can be and suggest ways in which you can progress in a systematic and sustainable way.

WHAT IS A REFLECTIVE PRACTITIONER?

In straightforward terms, a reflective practitioner is someone who is constantly questioning their practice and not content to take materials, strategies and ideas at face value but to examine them in their own context and decide what is best for the pupils in light of their reading and knowledge. The reflective practitioner also reflects on his or her own impact on the learning experience. We reflect in two ways: in-action and on-action. In other words, we reflect on our actions in 'real' time but also after the event in lesson evaluations, when we are driving home from work or marking exercise books.

By the time you have picked up this book, you will have started to develop a repertoire of approaches and some of them will be so automatic that you use them without thinking. Such craft knowledge has come to you from your own experience as a language learner, from your tutors, from observation of, and advice from, other teachers and from your reading. In time, we, as teachers, become far more confident in a variety of situations and, with experience, run the risk of being satisfied that we know *where* we are going and *what* we are doing. What we do not always know is *why* and *what* improvements could be made. Do we understand the underlying theory / theories? How does theory underpin our practice? There is a lot of truth in the saying that there is nothing more practical than good theory.

Activity 13.1

Respond to the statements below. Identify ways in which you (might) reflect. Tick the appropriate box(es) for each statement.

	I try to do this regularly but it is not always possible.	I would like to do this but never manage to do so.	This is not feasible given my role and responsibilities.	I don't think this is necessary.	I am not currently in a situation where I can do this but I would like to do it.	I'll try to do this in future.
1 I note down brief reflections on how the lesson has gone as soon as I can after the lesson.						
2 At the end of the day, I write up my reflections on the lessons.						
3 I focus on one class at a time and concentrate on getting that class right.						
4 I invite others to observe part or all of a lesson in order to get another perspective.						
5 I am always looking for new ideas in *Pathfinders* or other books or websites.						
6 I go to watch other teachers and learn from them.						
7 I ask pupils for their ideas and opinions.						
8 I visit other schools to find out how they do things.						

(Adapted from Race, 2005)

WHY BE A REFLECTIVE PRACTITIONER?

It follows that once our 'stage act' has become routine, it is all too easy to take things for granted and slip into a pattern. Why should we reflect and change?

1   We can all too easily stop learning and become hamsters on a wheel 'treading the same old treadmill' (see Lamb and Simpson, 2003: 55).
2   Reflection can increase our competence and understanding and increase our self-esteem, self-confidence, enthusiasm and, ultimately, job satisfaction.
3   As professionals, we have a moral responsibility to update our knowledge and skills and do our best to improve the quality of learning in the classroom.
4   We should model good practice in learning.
5   No two learning situations are the same. Our role is to maximise the learning experience by matching the strategies, materials and resources to the specific context.
6   Finally, we live in a rapidly changing world. Changes in terms of policy and practice are constants. Reflection and refreshment of ideas are essential.

How would you rank these arguments in terms of your own situation? Think about a specific aspect of your practice that you might too easily be 'taking for granted'.

Pachler and Field (2004) develop these ideas in Chapter 17 of *Starting to Teach in the Secondary School* where they discuss the benefits of continuing professional development (CPD).

Activity 13.2

Think about what motivates you as a teacher and what stimulates you to change and improve. Note down what you come up with and compare it with other teachers using the grid below.

	I strongly agree	I agree	Neither agree nor disagree	I disagree	I strongly disagree
I am motivated to reflect on my work and improve because I take a pride in my work.					
I rely on my experience and do not need to reflect in detail.					
I have not time to reflect so just get on with it.					
I am motivated to reflect on my work and improve because I am a professional.					
I rely on 'gut reaction' and this serves me well.					
I am motivated to reflect on my work and change because repetition bores me.					
I am motivated to reflect on my work because I take a pride in my work.					
I would reflect if I had time but for now I just get on with doing what I have to do.					
I am motivated to improve because I am afraid of failure.					

HOW CAN YOU REFLECT IN A MORE ORGANISED, SYSTEMATIC WAY?

It is one thing to say that you are going to be more reflective but it is another to undertake such a change. Here are some suggestions:

- having regular, timetabled (and sacrosanct!) mentoring sessions;
- keeping a journal;
- completing a portfolio of professional learning (for details see Field, 2002);
- conducting paired observation and paired planning.

Capel *et al.* (2001: Chapters 2.2, 5.4) develop these ideas in *Learning to Teach in the Secondary School*.

Activity 13.3

Identify the possible benefits of the following two approaches to discussing your practice.

1 You discuss your progress with your mentor/tutor/head of department on a weekly basis. Time is set aside for it and the agenda is yours. The 'mentor' always begins by asking what the high points of the week have been and then asks if there have been any problems. There is usually a specific focus to the meeting (oral work, target language, reading, homework) but sufficient flexibility to digress and talk about issues that have come up in the last week.

2 A group of teachers/students split into threes and are assigned a role: A, B or C. A describes his or her practice (on a set subject, e.g. flexible learning) for a set time (5–10 minutes). B listens but does not intervene at any time. C notes down the main points and the strategies. B then has 5 minutes to ask any questions which are simply designed to draw out more detail or to clarify issues. The roles are rotated such that at the end of 45 minutes, each teacher has been able to carry out all three roles. All three then discuss the issues that arise from the different descriptions of practice and, if they are part of a wider group, feed back in a plenary session.

One obvious way of reflecting is to engage in teacher research. This is dealt with in the next section.

HOW CAN RESEARCH HELP YOU?

You may have been involved in research during your studies and, hopefully, will have had the term demystified, the language of research explained and the benefits pointed out and experienced. If you have not, you may associate it with highly academic practices that are often done *to* teachers rather than *with* or *by* them. In a sense, we carry out research all the time, finding things out, checking information and ideas. What we normally fail to do is to do this systematically.

For classroom research to succeed, it arguably has to satisfy three conditions. It has to address an aspect of learning that:

- you want to change;
- you need to change;
- you are able to change.

Why the three conditions? Well, first of all, you have to have a desire to change something to see it through. Second, you must identify a genuine need to change or else, again, you will not carry it out. Third, it must be something that you can realistically change and it must be feasible. You may want and need to change Year 11's attitude to French, but how realistic is it for you to try to tackle that as a piece of research? What you must do is identify an area and, within that area, a specific intervention that will produce identifiable gains in performance whether it be attitude, behaviour or academic performance. This specific approach is called 'action research', also referred to as 'classroom research' or 'teacher research'.

Activity 13.4

Read the case study below and answer the following questions:

- What appear to be the essential characteristics of an action research cycle?
- What appear to be the steps in the process that must be followed?

Case study

A teacher of French in a secondary school was concerned about the impact that a teaching assistant (TA) was having on her lessons. The teacher who was using the target language was often interrupted by the TA reprimanding pupils in English for their behaviour. The focus of the intervention was to reduce the TA's use of English and encourage the use of French. The approach adopted was to involve the TA in language presentation at the beginning of each unit of work. The TA was given pronunciation practice and shown how to present the language.

The teacher decided to use audio recording to measure change and both she and the TA made diary entries. She began by recording the lesson to determine the extent of the problem.

The relatively simple intervention proved to be successful on a number of counts. The TA felt more involved and grew in confidence as she was perceived differently by the pupils. A professional dialogue was started on the subject of target language and the TA's role, and the interruptions ceased. The teacher went on to ask herself what else the TA could contribute in the target language and to the learning process generally.

ACTION RESEARCH CYCLE

Limitations of space prevent a detailed description and critique of the notion of 'action research' in this chapter. However, since action research embodies many of the good features of reflective practice and classroom-based research, it is worth summarising the main points and highlighting its strengths. Essentially, action research involves the following steps that must be followed (although not necessarily in strict order). Fundamentally, it must involve action (e.g. some change to practice, incorporation of new materials) and it must use research to inform practice:

- identify an area;
- define specific goals;
- develop a plan of work;
- develop your recording techniques (your research);
- evaluate success;

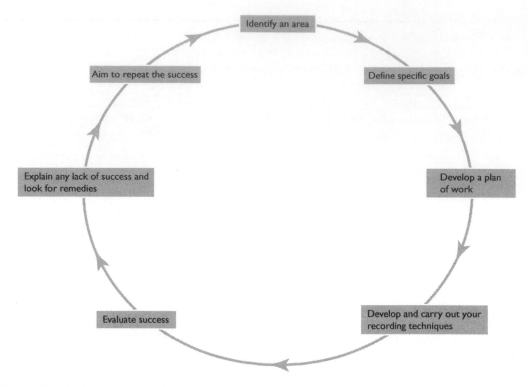

Figure 13.1 Action research cycle

- explain any lack of success and look for remedies;
- aim to repeat the success.

The cycle is often presented as a series of cycles or spirals. Central to the planning is the need to identify your goal. As the saying goes, if you do not know where you are going, any road will do and, I would add, you will not know when you get there. It is important to measure the impact of the change and evaluate it systematically rather than resort to 'gut reaction' as to whether a change has worked or not. The tighter the focus, the deeper the analysis and the greater the reflection.

Make sure the research is economical and try to involve others. The research will hopefully involve as many people as possible (including learners). The research tools will be chosen on their ability to give you the information that you need, not on the attractiveness or convenience of a particular method.

The analysis of evidence and evaluation are, in my experience, often the weakest elements. Action researchers are all too liable to run out of time, or steam, or both or be satisfied with their achievements without adequate reflection.

NB:

- Just because it is classroom based does not mean that it shouldn't be *rigorous*.
- It is not about knowing all the answers. *It's about asking better quality questions.* (See Hopkins, 2002.)

Activity 13.5

Fill in a potential action research cycle using the prompts.

Identify an area	*Which area of your teaching do you need to, want to and are able to change?*
Define specific goals	*What might be a very small, specific focus for you to work on?*
Develop a plan of work	*How long it is going to take? Which class(es)? Whose help are you going to enlist? What research and reconnaissance do you need to carry out first?*
Develop your recording techniques (your research in other words)	*How are you going to record and measure the change (observation, interview)?*
Evaluate success	*What have been the expected and unexpected outcomes?*
Explain any lack of success and look for remedies	*What has not quite worked to plan? Why is this? What could you do to put it right?*
Aim to repeat the success	*If it works with x, will it work with y? Can I extend the idea to other aspects? Can I share this with colleagues?*

WHAT THEN ARE THE BENEFITS OF REFLECTION AND RESEARCH?

Heilbronn (2004) talks of becoming 'research literate' and makes a more detailed case for research and its role in informing practice. The following are some of the benefits of reflection and research. They:

- provide us with the means to inform and change our practice;
- can motivate by providing us with stimulation and challenge;
- combine theory and practice and relate the former to the languages classroom in which we are working;
- empower us to take decisions on what we *know* to be right;
- give us the confidence to challenge new initiatives and assumptions and we become far less accepting of others' claims and published findings.

Activity 13.6

Identify sources to consult and actions that you can realistically take *now*.

For ideas and information:

- Bookmark and regularly visit key websites. For example:

  - www.linguanet.org.uk
  - www.vtc.ngfl.org.uk
  - www.cilt.org.uk
  - www.all-languages.org.uk

- Get hold of accessible books full of ideas and suggestions, for example through CILT.
- Join the Association for Language Learning as an active member and attend conferences and training events. Regularly read the Association's journals; for example, the *Language Learning Journal, Francophonie, Deutsch Lehren und Lernen, Vida Hispánica*.
- Get in touch with your local Comenius Centre and language organisation: *Goethe-Institut, Instituto Cervantes*, etc.

For action:

- Work out a sustainable pattern of reflection that suits you and stick to it.
- Try to involve colleagues or friends in the same or other institutions to work with you.
- Involve your pupils – they can surprise you with their insights!
- Find out about opportunities for accredited courses; for example Masters degree.
- Find out about any support/resources that might be available.

SUMMARY

At the outset, I identified you as someone who wants to extend your practice. You are, or have the potential to be, an 'extended professional', broadening the boundaries of your own practice. Hopefully, you will have a fruitful and challenging career in which you will never stop asking 'better quality questions'. Bon courage!

USEFUL WEBSITES

www.phil-race.com/files/reflection.doc
Phil Race is a well-known educator of the post-compulsory sector and his work on reflection including his extensive checklist is worth looking at.
www.jeanmcniff.com/booklet1.html
Jean McNiff is a leading writer on action research. This third edition of a short reader on action research is, in the spirit of much of the work of action researchers, a generous and thoughtful contribution to practice.
www.bath.ac.uk/~edsajw
Jack Whitehead is very well known for his work on action research. This website, based at the University of Bath, has a lot of information including the article above.
www.ncsl.org.uk/networked/index.cfm
NCSL have developed network communities that enable institutions to share good practice in terms of leadership and management. Other sites are recommended by them.
http://reflectingeducation.net
An interdisciplinary professional online journal of evidence-informed practice published by the WLE Centre for Excellence at the Institute of Education, University of London.
www.teachernet.gov.uk
Teachernet offers guidance on improving practice and also case studies of others who have been engaged in classroom-based research.

Bibliography

ACCAC/ National Assembly for Wales (2000) *Modern Foreign Languages in the National Curriculum in Wales.* Cardiff

Assessment Reform Group (2002) *Assessment for Learning: 10 Principles.* Available at www.assessment-reform-group.org.uk

Barnes, A. and Graham, S. (1997) *Target Language Testing.* Cheltenham: Stanley Thornes

Bell, S. (1998) *Storyline Scotland.* Available at www.storyline-scotland.freeserve.co.uk

Bessenyei, I. (2002) Internetgestützter Projektunterricht, in N. Pachler (ed.) *Lehren und Lernen mit Informatons- und Kommuniktionstechnologien.* Studienverlag: Innsbruck, pp. 153–180

Black, P., Harrison, C., Lee, C., Marshall, B. and Wiliam, D. (2003) *Assessment for Learning: Putting it into Practice.* Buckingham: Open University Press

Black, P. and Wiliam, D. (1998) *Inside the Black Box: Raising Standards Through Classroom Assessment.* London: King's College

Biriotti, L. (1999) *Grammar is Fun.* London: CILT

Block, D. (2002) Communicative language teaching revisited: discourses in conflict and foreign national teachers, *Language Learning Journal*, 26: 19–26

Bone, D. (1988) *A Practical Guide to Effective Listening.* London: Kogan Page

Buchanan, J. (2002) MFL beyond the classroom, in A. Swarbrick (ed.) *Aspects of Teaching Secondary Modern Foreign Languages: Perspectives on Practice.* London: RoutledgeFalmer

Buckby, M. (1980) *Action! Book 1.* Sunbury-on-Thames: Nelson

Cajkler, W. and Addelman, R. (1992) *The Practice of Foreign Language Teaching,* London: David Fulton

Capel, S., Leask, M. and Turner, T. (2001) *Learning to Teach in the Secondary School.* London: Routledge

Chambers G. (1993) Taking the de- out of demotivation, *Language Learning Journal*, 7: 1–6

Chambers, G. (1996) Listening. Why? How?, *Language Learning Journal*, 14: 23–7

Chambers, G. (1998) Pupils' perceptions of the foreign language learning experience, *Language Teaching Research*, 2(3): 231–59

Chambers, G. (1999) *Motivating Language Learners.* Clevedon: Multilingual Matters Ltd

Chambers, G. and Pearson, S. (2004) 'If only we had the time!' Perceptions of teachers and the TAs with whom they work, *Language Learning Journal*, 29: 32–41

Chang, S. (2004) The roles of mentors in electronic learning environments, *AACE Journal*, 12(3): 331–42

Collins, M. and Berge, Z. (1996) Facilitating interaction in computer mediated online courses, background information paper for a presentation at the *FSU/AECT Distance Education Conference*, Tallahassee, Fl. Available at www.emoderators.com/moderators/flcc.html

Coyle, D. (2002) Towards a reconceptualization of the MFL curriculum, in A. Swarbrick (ed.)

Teaching Modern Foreign Languages in Secondary Schools. London: RoutledgeFalmer, pp. 156–72

Dahlhaus, B. (1994) *Fertigkeit Hören.* Langenscheidt: Berlin/München

DES/WO (1990) *Modern Foreign Languages for Ages 11 to 16.* London: HMSO

DfEE (1998) *The National Literacy Strategy. Framework for Teaching.* London: DfEE

DfEE/QCA (1999) *The National Curriculum for England: Modern Foreign Languages.* London. Available at www.nc.uk.net

DfES (2000) *Supporting the Teaching Assistant: A Good Practice Guide.* London. Available at www.teachernet.gov.uk/remodelling

DfES (2002a) *Languages for All: Languages for Life. A Strategy for England.* London. Available at www.dfes.gov.uk/languagesstrategy/pdf/DfESLanguagesStrategy.pdf

DfES (2002b) *Literacy in Modern Foreign Languages.* London

DfES (2003a) *Foundation Subjects MFL: Core Training Materials.* London

DfES (2003b) *Key Stage 3 National Strategy. Framework for Teaching Modern Foreign Languages: Years 7, 8 and 9.* London. Available at www.standards.dfes.gov.uk/keystage3/respub/mflframework

DfES (2004) *Five-Year Strategy for Children and Learners. Putting People at the Heart of Public Services.* London. Available at www.dfes.gov.uk/publications/5yearstrategy/docs/DfES5Yearstrategy.pdf

DfES (2005a) *Common Core of Skills and Knowledge for the Children's Workforce.* Non-statutory guidance. London. Available at: www.dfes.gov.uk/commoncore/docs/5610_COMMON CORE.pdf

DfES (2005b) *The Key Stage 2 Framework for Languages.* London. Available at www.standards. dfes.gov.uk/primary/publications/languages/framework/

DfES *et al.* (2003) *Raising Standards and Tackling Workload: A National Agreement. Time for Standards.* January 15

Driscoll, P., Jones, J. and Macrory, G. (2004) *The Provision of Foreign Language Learning for Pupils at Key Stage 2.* Available at www.dfes.gov.uk/languages

Edexcel (2003) *Specification, GCSE in French* (1226)

Fehse, K. and Kocher, D. (2002) Storyline projects in the foreign language classroom, in O. Kühn and O. Mentz (eds) *Zwischen Kreativität, Konstruktion und Emotion: Der etwas andere Fremdsprachenuntericht.* Centaurus Verlag

Field, K. (ed.) (2000) *Issues in Modern Foreign Languages Teaching.* London: RoutledgeFalmer

Field, K. (2002) *Portfolio of Professional Development: Structuring and Recording Teachers' Career Development.* London: Optimus Publishing

Graham, S. (1997) *Effective Language Learning.* Clevedon: Multilingual Matters

Graham, S. (2002) Experiences of learning French: a snapshot at Years 11, 12 and 13, *Language Learning Journal*, 25: 15–20

Grauberg, W. (1997) *The Elements of Foreign Language Teaching.* Clevedon: Multilingual Matters

Harris, V. and Snow, D. (2004) *Doing It for Themselves: Focus on Learning Strategies and Vocabulary Building.* London: CILT

Harris, V., Burch, J., Jones, B. and Darcy, J. (2001) *Something to Say?* London: CILT

Hawkins, E. (1987) *Modern Languages in the Curriculum.* Cambridge: Cambridge University Press

Hawkins, E. (1994) Percept before precept, in L. King and P. Boaks (eds) *Grammar! A Conference Report.* London: CILT, pp. 109–23

Heilbronn, R. (2004) Using research and evidence to inform your teaching, in S. Capel, R. Heilbronn, M. Leask and T. Turner (eds) *Starting to Teach in the Secondary School.* Second edition. London: RoutledgeFalmer, pp. 221–32

Hopkins, D. (2002) *A Teacher's Guide to Classroom Research.* Third edition. Buckingham: Open University Press

Johnstone, R. (1994) *Teaching Modern Languages at Primary School – Approaches and Implications.* Edinburgh: Scottish Council for Research in Education

Jones, B. (1992) *Exploring Otherness. An Approach to Cultural Awareness*. London: CILT

Jones, B. (2000) Developing cultural awareness, in K. Field (ed.) *Issues in Modern Foreign Languages Teaching*. London: Routledge, pp. 158–70

Jones, J. (2000) Teaching grammar in the Modern Foreign Language classroom, in K. Field (ed.) *Issues in Modern Foreign Languages Teaching*. London: Routledge Falmer, pp.142–57

Lamb, T. and Simpson, M. (2003) Escaping from the treadmill: practitioner research and professional autonomy, *Language Learning Journal*, 28: 55–63

Lawes, S. (2000) The unique contribution of Modern Foreign Languages to the curriculum, in K. Field (ed.) *Issues in Modern Foreign Languages Teaching*. London: Routledge, pp. 87–98

Leask, M. and Pachler, N. (2005) *Learning to Teach Using ICT in the Secondary School*. Second edition. London: RoutledgeFalmer

Lightbown, P. (2003) SLA research in the classroom/SLA research for the classroom, *Language Learning Journal*, 28: 4–13

Littlewood, W. (1981) *Communicative Language Teaching*. Cambridge: Cambridge University Press

Low, L., Brown, S., Johnstone, R. and Pirrie, A. (1995) *Foreign Languages in Primary Schools: Evaluation of the Scottish pilot projects 1993–5*. Final report to Scottish Office. Stirling: Scottish CILT

Macaro, E. (2000) Issues in target language teaching, in K. Field (ed.) *Issues in Modern Foreign Language Teaching*. London: Routledge, pp. 175–93

Macaro, E. (2001) Analysing student teachers' codeswitching in foreign language classrooms: theories and decision making, *The Modern Language Journal*, 85(4): 531–48

Macaro, E. (2003) *Teaching and Learning a Second Language*. London: Continuum

Macdonald, C. (1993) *Using the Target Language*. Cheltenham: Mary Glasgow Publications/ ALL

March, T. (1998) Why webquests? An introduction. Available at www.ozline.com/ webquests/intro.html

Martin, C. and Cheater, C. (1998) *Let's Join In! Rhymes, Poems and Songs*. London: CILT

Mary Glasgow Publications (1983) *Bibliobus*. London: Mary Glasgow Publications.

Mary Glasgow Publications (1986) *Lesekiste*. London: Mary Glasgow Publications.

Meiring, L. and Norman, N. (2001) Grammar in MFL teaching revisited, in *Language Learning Journal*, 23: 58–66

Meiring, L. and Norman, N. (2002) Back on target: repositioning the status of target language, in MFL teaching and learning, *Language Learning Journal*, 26: 27–35

Mittergeber, M. (2004) Interessante WebQuests – Lernabenteuer im Internet, *Tel&Cal 1/04*, pp. 44–8. Available at www.eduhi.at/dl/0812.pdf

Morgan, C. and Neil, P. (2001) *Teaching Modern Foreign Languages. A Handbook for Teachers*. London: Kogan Page

NALA/Central Bureau (1992) *The Foreign Language Assistant: A Guide to Good Practice*. London: Central Bureau

Neather, T. (2003) *Getting to Grips with Grammar*. London: CILT

OFSTED (1999–2000; 2000–2001) *Secondary Subject Reports for Modern Foreign Languages*. London. Available at www.ofsted.gov.uk

OFSTED (2004) *OFSTED subject Reports 2002/3. Modern Foreign Languages in Secondary Schools*. London: HMI. Available at www.ofsted.gov.uk/publications/docs/3542.doc

Pachler, N. (2000) Re-examining communicative language teaching, in K. Field (ed.) *Issues in Modern Foreign Languages Teaching*. London: Routledge/Falmer, pp. 22–37

Pachler, N. (ed.) (1999) *Teaching Modern Foreign Languages at Advanced Level*. London: Routledge

Pachler, N. and Field, K. (2001) *Learning to Teach Modern Foreign Languages in the Secondary School. A Companion to School Experience*. Second edition. London: Routledge

Pachler, N. and Field, K. (2004) Continuing professional development, in S. Capel,

R. Heilbronn, M. Leask and T. Turner (eds) *Starting to Teach in the Secondary School.* Second edition. London: RoutledgeFalmer, pp. 233–46

Phipps, W. (1999) *Pairwork: Interaction in the Modern Languages Classroom.* London: CILT

Poole, B. (1999) Is younger better? – A critical examination of the beliefs about learning a foreign language at primary school. Unpublished PhD thesis. Institute of Education, University of London

Powell, B., Wray, D., Rixon, S., Medwell J., Barnes, A. and Hunt, M. (2001) *Analysis and Evaluation of the Current Situation Relating to the Teaching of Modern Foreign Languages at Key Stage 2 in England.* QCA. Available at www.qca.org.uk/ca/subjects/mfl/warwick.pdf

Race, P. (2005) *Making Learning Happen.* London: Sage

Rendall, H. (1998) *Stimulating Grammatical Awareness. A Fresh Look at Language Acquisition.* London: CILT

Sato, K. and Kleinsasser, R. (1999) Communicative language teaching (CLT): practical understandings, *The Modern Language Journal*, 83(4): 494–517

Scullard, S. (1990) *Abgemacht! Pairwork Activities in German.* Cheltenham

Seeger, H. (1985) *Wer? Wie? Was?* 1, Schülerbuch, VUB Printmedia Gmbtt, Abt. Gilde Verlag, p. 56.

Skarbek, C. (1998) *First Steps to Reading and Writing.* London: CILT

Snow, D. and Byram, M. (1997) *Crossing Frontiers: The School Study Visit Abroad.* London: CILT

Solmecke, G. (1992) Ohne Hören kein Sprechen, *Fremsprache Deutsch*, 7: 4–11

Swarbrick, A. (ed.) (1994) *Teaching Modern languages.* London: The Open University

Swarbrick, A. (ed.) (2002) *Teaching Modern Foreign Languages in Secondary School.* London: RoutledgeFalmer

Truss, Lynne (2003) *Eats, Shoots and Leaves: The Zero Tolerance Approach to Punctuation.* London: Profile Books

Turner, K. (1995) *Listening in a Foreign Language. A Skill we Take for Granted?* London: CILT

Underwood, M. (1989) *Teaching Listening.* Longman: London

Ur, P. (1996) *A Course in Language Teaching: Practice and Theory.* Cambridge: Cambridge University Press

White, G. (2001) *Listening.* Oxford: Oxford University Press

Index

An environmentally friendly book printed and bound in England by www.printondemand-worldwide.com

#0676 - - C0 - 297/210/8 - PB